A NEW PARTY FOR SOCIALISM

– WHY? HOW? WHEN?

By whom? On what programme?

Answers to some burning questions – and some new questions

By Cliff Slaughter

Workers Revolutionary Party (Workers Press)

Published 1996 by Workers Revolutionary Party (Workers Press)
PO Box 735, London SW8 1YB.

Typeset by Sumner Type, London SE22
Printed by Trade Union Printing Services, Newcastle-upon-Tyne

A C.I.P. catalogue record for this book is available from the British Library

ISBN: 1-871518-15-6

CONTENTS

1	INTRODUCTORY - the Labour Party and after	1
2	National or International	24
3	Capitalism Yesterday and Today	32
4	Towards the Socialist Offensive	43
5	Party and Programme	46
6	Programme and Party	61
7	What Kind of Party?	68
8	The 'New Party' and the WRP	74
9	The Next Steps	81
Appendix I: The Basic Lines of our Work		88
Appendix II: Marxism and the working class today		93
Reclaim the Future		99

1

INTRODUCTORY — the Labour Party and after

Why a new party?

THE working class needs a new party. Why is this idea becoming more and more widespread?

Because the Labour Party is moving farther and farther away from the working class which founded it nearly 100 years ago. Blair and his team are remote from working people and their mounting problems.

They have removed Clause Four ('common ownership of the means of production, distribution and exchange') from the Party's Constitution. They support the anti-trade union laws, yet the Labour Party was formed above all to protect the legal independence and rights of unions. They make their appeal to the better-off sections of the middle class and to big business. They have abandoned the aim of full employment. They have entirely different standards for themselves than they do for the working people they expect to vote for them, in terms of wages, health-care, and of course education: witness the blatant hypocrisy of Blair and Harman in choosing their children's schools.

People have a growing sense that big changes are necessary if their problems are to be solved, and they see a Labour Party which is now completely adapted to the capitalist *status quo*. What alternative is there? In the past, convinced socialists sometimes turned to the Communist Party as an alternative. But since 1989, the Stalinist bureaucracy in the Soviet Union and elsewhere, and the system they controlled, have totally collapsed, and the Communist Party is no more. In any case, Stalinist bureaucratic abuses and atrocities had for many years done more than any anti-communist propaganda to discredit the Communist Party's politics.

But in considering the need for a new party and how to get it, we have to go deeper than these immediate perceptions. First of all, we need a thorough study and explanation of the historical reasons for the present crisis in the labour movement. It is no answer just to proclaim a new 'socialist' Labour party, as Arthur Scargill has done.

The second thing that needs to be said is that the new party for socialism the working class so urgently needs will not come into being just through argument and explanation, let alone by proclamation. It can come into existence only on the basis of big movements, mass struggles, big shocks. Only through such experience will the working class - or a significant section of it - give up the mass political party which brought it into political life, the Labour Party. No doubt we can expect that the attacks on the working class which the coming Labour Government will inevitably make will provide just such experiences. So those who already see the necessity of building a new party, and are prepared to accept that responsibility, must above all carefully prepare for those attacks over the next two or three years, and particularly in the months immediately ahead. This pamphlet aims to be part of that preparation.

THE problem of a new party did not arise yesterday. Seventy years ago the working classes not only of Britain but all over the world needed new parties. The 'socialist' parties had already gone over to their 'own' capitalist ruling classes in the 1914-18 war, and ever after were used as instruments of rule over their own supporters, the working classes. The Communist Parties, formed after the Russian Revolution of October 1917, became, first, the victims of the 'socialism in one country' dead-end of Stalin and the bureaucracy, and afterwards, under

INTRODUCTION

the illusion that they were defending socialism in the Soviet Union, advocates of 'peaceful coexistence with capitalism' and defenders of the Stalinist tyranny. Now, their remnants have openly gone over to the politics of the 'socialist' or 'social-democratic' traitors. Men and women who joined those parties to be communists, internationalists will be among the forces who build a new party.

For 70 years the followers of Leon Trotsky - who was exiled and then assassinated by Stalin's agents in 1940 - defended Marxism and the aims of internationalism and socialist revolution against these false leaders. They explained that this crisis of working-class leadership must be resolved, as the key to the crisis of all humanity caused by capitalism's decay.

The difference now is this: today, the need for a new party is beginning to become clear to far wider circles of people. Following the collapse of the Soviet bureaucracy, the Communist Parties have collapsed, as in Britain, or become 'social-democratic', as in Italy. The Labour Party and its 'socialist' equivalents in other countries have now openly abandoned any socialist aims and are in the last stage of severing their connection with the organised workers in their trade unions. There is no solution except socialism to the massive problems of unemployment, homelessness, destruction of welfare services, health-care and education, destruction of the environmnent, and the recurrence of fascist reaction and war. And yet the parties founded by the working class finally renounce socialism.

A new party is needed, and this will more and more be seen by thousands and thousands of people.

Who will found this new party?

THE Workers Revolutionary Party, like all the existing groups calling themselves Trotskyist, was formed in the particular conditions of the domination of the world working-class movement by Stalinism. This has meant that Trotskyist organisations, necessarily 'swimming against the stream', remained small and to a great extent isolated from the mass of workers, who remained supporters of the traditional working-class parties.

The new party that the working class needs must, on the contrary, have membership from and influence upon significant sections of the class. Such parties are formed only in the course of big struggles, experiences, challenges and shocks for the working class as a class. We have now entered a period in which such struggles and shocks are being inescapably prepared because of the historical, structural crisis of the whole capitalist system. And already one of the effects of this profound crisis is that Stalinism has collapsed and Labourism has revealed its final bankruptcy.

Some socialists fear that this collapse of the 'traditional' parties weakens the working class as it comes to confront the struggles ahead. They say that it is a very unfavourable time to be working for a new party. The very opposite is true.

It is of course true that Stalinism and social-democracy (Labourism) have done enormous damage to the class movement of the working class, to its organisation and consciousness. But it is the years of their domination, not their collapse, that have done that damage! The working class now goes into a period of imminent struggles and shocks in which socialists, Marxists, have the responsibility of taking part in the building of new parties and organisations of working-class struggle, in a situation where Stalinism is dead and Labourism, proving itself finally bankrupt as a reformist party, will spearhead capital's attack.

There are those who pull back from this responsibility on the grounds that 'working-class consciousness is damaged' or 'the working-class movement is at a low ebb, the situation is unfavourable', or 'we see no new forces, no signs of a reconstruction of the working-class movement', or 'the Stalinists still retain a certain hold over the working class, though in different forms', and so on. Those who say things like this are missing their time in history. They are falling victim to that ideological pressure of the middle-class 'intellectuals' who cannot see beyond the horizons of capitalism, and who are retailing the ideological message of the ruling class: 'Socialism has failed; Marxism is dead'.

It should come as no surprise that some who consider themselves Marxists, looking at the smallness of the forces they have been able to build and retain in the long years of relative isolation imposed by Stalinism, draw the conclusion that the forces for a new party able to bid for leadership of the working class do not yet exist.

They make the mistake of not turning their eyes, their thinking and feeling to the masses of working people who have urgent needs which the Labour Party can in no way satisfy - people who are most certainly being forced into movement, who will experience great historic shocks to their existing way of life and consciousness. They now begin to provide the living 'culture' within which the working class will become conscious of what it must aim at, how it must organise. Thousands of individuals will come forward to organise, coordinate, inspire and lead their fellow men and women.

No one to form a new party? There are thousands of people to form a new party! Mohammed must go to the mountain! That is what the Marxists must learn - now!

IT IS a fact that for scores of years, until now, the job of Marxists has been first of all to organise and speak out as Trotskyists against the betrayals by the Stalinist and Labour leaders, and to fight for the continuity of Marxism, of working-class internationalism, grasping what few opportunities there were for getting close to the struggles of the working class.

But now, unless the Marxists can immerse themselves in the movements, the struggles, the thinking, of all those driven into action by the universal crisis of capitalist economy, society and culture, they have no future, only a noble past. The only *raison d'être* of the Trotskyists today is to fight their way out of isolation, to subordinate every relation between ourselves to the vital one, the life-and-death one, namely, that we must be bound together indissolubly by the decision to break out, to be the most disciplined and determined fighters for banding together a new party of the working class for socialism.

This is not done by proclamation but by hard, organising work over a lengthy period, by putting all our political resources at the disposal of the new forces who are now coming forward, so that they can forge themselves into a new party. Like all others who are coming forward, we have to fight night and day to show the necessary socialist direction of all the many struggles and demands now coming up, many of them not immediately or 'in themselves' socialist at all.

Old ways of thinking, in this regard, have to be overcome. It is not a question of 'intervening' in struggles, or 'politicising' them or, 'conscientising' them, as it is fashionable to say in some 'left' circles. The aim is to make these struggles more effective and, where possible, successful - to find ways of supporting them, so that they become part of a new reconstructed, self-movement of the working class as a class.

The legacy of Stalinism and Labourism has to be negated and overcome, because by their nature - bureaucratic, anti-internationalist, authoritarian and against all initiative from below - Stalinism and Labourism were entirely opposed to this self-movement of the working class.

The Labour Party: one step forward, one hundred steps back.

THE Labour Party was never a socialist party. It has had, and still has, socialists in it. But it has always been a party tied to the British state, to the capitalist system which that state defends, and to the parliamentary system through which it governs.

When the Labour Party was formed, it represented potentially a big step forward for the British working class. Its aims were not defined as socialist; it was organised for purely parliamentary politics and was formed so that the trade unions

INTRODUCTION

could have their independence and resources protected by legislation, through labour representation in parliament. Yet in the shape of the Labour Party the organised working-class movement entered politics, taking a step to confronting the employers politically, as a class.

Whether this first step could lead to the actual political independence of the working class from its class enemy, capital, was not yet decided.

The Labour Party is a party of the capitalist state. Blair now openly boasts of this when he says: 'Labour is the party of government'. At the same time, the Labour Party has been the party of the British working class for the whole of the 20th century. Is this not a contradiction? Yes, it is: a living contradiction. The Labour Party is a bourgeois workers' party, i.e., a capitalist workers' party.

HOW is the situation different today, such that it provides the conditions in which we call for a new party to replace Labour?

The difference has deep historical roots. It was the special powerful position of a few great capitalist powers from the beginning of this century that gave the ruling capitalist class in those countries the wealth to control the working class. By about 1900 the workers had built powerful trade unions and, in most European countries, political parties. Capitalism in Britain, Germany, France and the USA, with Russia just coming on the scene, had entered its new and highest stage, imperialism.

As capital became more centralised and concentrated, monopoly, mergers and cartels more and more replaced competition. Merging with industrial capital, finance capital and the banks became dominant. To the world market in exported goods was added the export of capital.

The few great imperialist powers divided the world among themselves. By subjecting their colonies and dependencies to super-exploitation, the metropolitan countries accumulated vast wealth. Wars for the division and re-division of the world became inevitable.

At the beginning of the 20th century Britain was in a very

strong position in this new world of imperialism. It had a massive colonial empire. British capitalism had been first on the world scene, and still dominated industrially as well as commercially and financially in the world market. This great wealth and power enabled the British ruling class to buy off one generation of Labour and trade union leaders after another. It was not only a matter of personal corruption, or of these leaders succumbing, as they did, to the ideology and the privileges of 'British' greatness.

Out of its imperialist super-profits the capitalist class could afford to allow a certain bargaining strength and a certain differential in living standards to a significant layer of skilled and organised workers. On this privileged layer the Labour and trade union bureaucracy rested, steadily becoming integrated into the capitalist state apparatus. The same reservoir of imperial wealth enabled the capitalist class from time to time to pacify and control the mass of workers by granting certain limited concessions and reforms, not only through trade union bargaining but also through legislation carried out by Labour Governments.

These are the material foundations of the Labour Party's ability to tie the British working class down to a position in which its great organised strength has been contained, to the great advantage of capital. The whole Labour bureaucratic and parliamentary apparatus has been built on the possibility of holding out for relatively long periods the real prospect of gradual gains through legislated reforms on a narrow national basis. This apparatus has gained a grip on the working-class movement, time and again stifling the socialist aspirations and attempts to organise of those who have taken the lead in working-class struggles.[1]

During and after World War I, British imperialism rapidly lost

---

[1] There was a brief interlude, following the 1917 October Russian Revolution and World War I, when the shop stewards' movement and other militant workers joined with Marxist organisations to found an alternative, the Communist Party. But by the end of 1924 the world's Communist Parties fell victim to the Stalinist line of 'socialism in a single country (Russia)'. And so when in 1926 the great industrial strength of the British working class came forward in the General Strike with the possibility and necessity of politically challenging the capitalist state, Stalin's faction imposed on the young Communist Party an opportunist line of refusing that challenge, leaving the TUC General Council free to betray the strike. Time and again between 1926 and 1990, when the Communist Parties disintegrated, the British Communist Party smoothed the path for the continued domination of the Labour and TUC leaders.

INTRODUCTION

its leading world position and went into decline, while US capitalism established itself as the dominant power. In the great depression of the 1930s, Britain's decline seemed irreversible. The crisis seemed terminal. The MacDonald government's attacks on the unemployed foreshadowed the Labour Party's preparations 65 years later for taking back gains won by the working class in the past.

On the basis of the world boom in trade and production which followed the devastation of World War II, the British capitalist class was able to ride the storm caused in 1945 by a working class which wanted to ensure that 'never again!' would it return to the Hungry Thirties. There was no avoiding the election of a Labour Government. This nationalised a few run-down industries, giving massive compensation to the owners and structuring the industries so that they served private enterprise on very favourable terms and, moreover, could be modernised and prepared for resale to the private sector at a future date. The Labour government also implemented health, educational and unemployment reforms. But it posed not the slightest challenge to the power of the state or of capital.

GERMAN and Japanese imperialism, though defeated in World War II, were within a few short years far in advance of Britain. But the boom years of the 1950s and 1960s to some extent concealed Britain's continuing decline. Illusions were rife. Academics and Labour politicians alike decided that capitalism had overcome its contradictions - whose existence they had in any case always denied. Stalinists and others in retreat from revolutionary Marxism decided that there could be centuries of 'peaceful coexistence' between capitalism and Stalinism, each armed to the teeth with nuclear weapons and calling themselves respectively, without a tinge of embarrassment, 'the Free World' and 'Socialism'.

In fact, the 'globalisation' that was going on was simply the frenzied rush - especially by the USA, which emerged from World War II as a 'superpower' - to exhaust all the possibilities of capitalist expansion and of displacing capitalism's contradictions. This is why from the early 1970s onwards there has developed a universal economic, social and political crisis of the system.

Then began the period of reaction all along the line. The fact that anti-union laws have been enacted in every capitalist country since then is not an accident. It is the stark recognition by capital's representatives that the system will no longer be able to coexist with a working class which uses its organised srength to force economic concessions. In other words, capital must be free to decide the price of labour-power without let or hindrance.

The same goes for 'full employment' and the whole structure called the welfare state, by which the capitalist class, working through its 'labour lieutenants', ensured enough political consensus by granting welfare reforms. What the capitalist spokespersons call 'the fiscal (taxation) crisis of the state' comes from the same source: it means that the payment of taxes out of the capitalists' income to finance state benefits to sustain the old, the sick, the unemployed, can no longer be afforded.

Could there be a surer sign of the system's historical bankruptcy - that it cannot afford to keep people alive? Yet the last half-century's conquests of science and technique, and the previously unimaginable increase in the productivity of labour, are the potential basis for universal prosperity! But capitalism now requires that the gains of the past must go. Just as Labour gave capital what it required when reforms were the way to control the working class, so now 'new Labour' must give capital what it requires. It must implement the attacks needed by the employing class. It must play its part in taking back the gains of all past struggles.

That is the meaning of 'new Labour', its renunciation of Clause Four, its acceptance and intended enforcement of the anti-union laws, its abandonment of 'full employment', its claim to be 'the party of law and order', 'the party of government'.

AS WE shall see below, the fight back against all this, which has

INTRODUCTION

already begun during the period of Tory rule, will mean the working class coming into conflict with its own traditional party in government. It will be a hard fight. A future Labour Government will conduct the offensive which capital requires against the working class and against all the conditions it has won in the past.

But even though the working class's fight begins as a defensive one, the relationship of forces will be in its favour. The material basis of the Labour Party's parliamentary and reformist control over the working-class movement in Britain - that is, the strength of British imperialism and the renewed ability of capitalism as a whole to displace its contradictions and afford concessions when necessary - no longer exists. Moreover, the Stalinist bureaucracy which came to imperialism's aid, and was the main barrier between the working class and Marxism, no longer exists either.

Marxists long ago anticipated these changes. But to these must be added a powerful social change to the advantage of the working class as the force for socialism. The attacks of capital on security of employment, its drive for productivity and 'rationalisation', its increasingly ruthless imposition of the demands of finance capital against the interests of millions of 'small people', its 'deregulation' which destroys traditional agreements and privileges - all this has had drastic effects on millions of men and women in Britain and the major capitalist countries who thought they could be sure of a settled and respectable life and status somewhere above the ordinary working classes. Together with the 'labour aristocracy' of skilled and better-paid workers in the traditional industries, this social stratification was the social base of Labourism.

'New Labour' cultivates the illusion that it can appeal to 'middle England', but the reality is that the social base of Labourism is crumbling. The workers who have always voted for Labour will be forced to fight against it and reject it. And now millions who in their conditions of life, relative security, social status and ideology had tended to become separated from the life of the proletariat and its movement, are forced to recognise that they are not spared the consequences of capital's attack any more than is the working class as a whole.

Thus the conditions are maturing for a truly mass movement of resistance to capital's attacks, for this movement to come into conflict with a Labour Government, and for a real break with the Labour Party, to a new socialist working-class party.

According to Marx's original theories, capital polarises the two main classes, driving the middle strata down into the proletariat, increasing the latter's ranks and social weight. It could be said that this process now revisits capitalism in a new and surprising way. Those whom sociologists and economists once liked to call the 'new middle classes' are now just as inexorably driven to accept their position as part of the working class!

Trade unions, the Labour Party, and the new party

BLAIR is taking steps to 'free' the Parliamentary Labour Party, the Party machine, and himself as Labour leader and future Prime Minister, from any dependence on the trade unions. As well as recommending him and 'new Labour' to the employers, he sees this as freeing his hands for future use of the anti-union laws against the working class and, he hopes, as a vote-winner among people who previously voted Conservative.

It is a crude operation and at the same a delicate one, because Blair needs, for the time being at least, to keep the source of money provided by the trade unions' political funds and to have the political support of the union bureaucracy in controlling their members. At more than one trade union annual conference in 1995, Blair laid down the law about a strict division of labour: the unions must stick to defending their members' conditions of work, and the Labour Party will do the governing or conduct the political opposition. Keep out of politics, leave it to the professionals, is the message to the unions and to the workers in them. This is, after all, a big question for Blair's whole project.

INTRODUCTION

It is important to remember that the relation between trade unions and party developed differently in Britain and in the other countries of Europe. Here, trade unions existed long before the founding of the Labour Party, and were then responsible for that founding in 1900-1906.[2] On the Continent, working-class political parties existed before national trade unions, and in some countries (e.g. France) different parties are associated with separate trade union federations.

This difference was closely linked to the fact that British capitalism was first in the field. The early socialist movements of the industrial working class in the first half of the nineteenth century, especially Chartism, gave way to a period of the development of trade unions as Britain's rapid industrial growth took off following the defeat of the 1848 revolutions in mainland Europe. When eventually the Labour Party was founded it was as a result of a pragmatic decision, based on hard experience, to ensure independent representation in parliament to protect trade unions - a very different thing from deciding to form a party on the sound theoretical basis of the necessity of organising for working-class political power and socialism.

This pragmatic, 'trade unionist' and non-theoretical character of the labour movement - in its great majority, and always in its leadership - has been a permanent weakness, inhibiting the building of alternative leadership and restricting the often highly militant struggles of sections of the working class to narrow horizons which prevented their victory. The most general and 'practical' manifestation of this weakness is the separation between what are called the political and industrial wings of the labour movement. This division is not at all something new, proposed by Blair (who only wants to take it to its extreme), but something imposed on the movement for a whole century and something which has been of inestimable advantage to the ruling class - and of course to the right-wing leaders of both the Labour Party and the trade unions. This

---

[2] As the result of socialist initiative at the 1899 TUC, the Labour Representation Committee was formed in February 1900 as a federation of trades unions and socialist societies. Following the 1906 General Election, in which 29 of its parliamentary candidates were elected, the LRC changed its name to Labour Party.

division keeps out of politics the organised strength of the working class in the workplace. That is to say, the organised strength of the working class cannot be brought to bear against the employers as a class. Labour cannot counter capital as such with its own organised strength.

Through their unions, workers are restricted to organising against their individual employer, or against the employers of a particular trade or industry at the most. Yet at the same time, the bureaucratised leaders of the unions are left free to use the unions' resources to merge, as they have done, with the right-wing leadership and apparatus of the Labour Party, strengthening it through the bloc vote they have wielded at party conferences, through the sponsoring and nomination of MPs, and through financial subsidies.

Thus, while the unionised workers themselves have been cut off from political influence by the 'industrial-political' divide, their bureaucratic leaders have mightily reinforced the right-wing, bourgeois grip of the Labour leaders on working-class politics. These same leaders operate entirely within the framework of the capitalist state and more and more directly as part of that apparatus; this is by far the most important political weapon of the ruling class for the control of labour.

The working class therefore needs urgently to overcome the imposed division between its 'industrial and political wings'. But that does not mean to say that socialists should ignore or oppose political work in elections and in parliament. What needs to be rejected is the idea that the working class has no political role except to break up into its millions of individual voting units and vote representatives into parliament. The working class needs above all to concentrate its strength politically, not fragment it into individual decisions once every five years or so!

For a working-class party fighting for socialism, participation in elections and in parliament will be important, but only in order to raise everywhere the main political questions of how to defeat the ruling class, to speak 'over the heads' of

INTRODUCTION

parliament to the working class nationally and internationally, to expose the workings of the capitalist state including parliament itself and the bourgeois political parties. The most important thing will be to make sure that in whatever issues and struggles people are involved, their fight is echoed and strengthened by a fight in parliament also.

As against such a fight, the Labour leaders insist on a Parliamentary Party which is 'independent' of the unions - they mean, independent of the working class, independent of those who voted for them, and free to make its own relations with the ruling class, its representatives and its state. Explaining his idea of the Labour Party as 'the party of government', Blair has said he will govern on behalf of the nation and not of any 'vested interest'. By vested interest, he explained, he meant not the interests of big capital but trade unions! What he meant was that 'new Labour' can be relied upon to subordinate the working class politically to the requirements of the capitalist state and the Labour leaders' own position within it.

But it would be a mistake to think that Blair's determination to serve the capitalist state directly and deny any political strength to the workers in their trade unions is something new. Certainly it is more open and blatant now, with Labour's acceptance of the anti-union laws. Yet, if we understand the aim of the working-class movement as it should be understood - the self-movement of the class to socialism - then we see that the fatal separation of the 'industrial and political wings of the movement' is as old as the Labour Party itself.

SO OUR aim, in working for the founding of a new party, cannot be to revive something like 'old Labour', as Arthur Scargill mistakenly thinks, with its parliamentary politics and trade union affiliations - even if that were possible. Scargill and those who propose to found the Socialist Labour Party correctly drew the conclusion from the 1984-85 miners' strike, which became a battle against the state, that a new socialist party was necessary.

But they have given the wrong answer to the question: what

kind of party? And this is because so far they have not gone deeply enough into an analysis of the roots of the relation between the Labour Party and capitalist rule. Such an analysis goes against the grain of the 'English dislike of theory'. But here Marxist theory is absolutely necessary. What looks like a 'common-sense' division of labour between parliamentary politics and the work of trade unions is in fact, as we have seen, an acceptance of the terms dictated by the rule of capital.

So far as capital and its representatives are concerned, the working class is nothing more than a naturally existing mass of individual repositories of labour-power which can be employed and made to turn out values which render a profit - objects, employed by capital. Karl Marx showed that the working class is much, much more than that.

First, the working class does not exist 'naturally' but came into existence by the forcible dispossession and removal from the land of the working population at the beginning of the capitalist epoch, more than two centuries ago.

Second, the working class is not just an employed and exploited class; it is the class of men and women whose labour provides the basis for the life and culture of the whole of humanity, and this now gives it a unique historical role.

Such is the productivity of labour today, using the conquests of science and the interconnectedness of the labours of the people of all nations, that it could provide prosperity and freedom and a creative life for all. But while production is subordinated to exploitation and profit and not to human need - something which capital cannot avoid - this uncontrolled exploitation only plunders and threatens to destroy the planet entirely, and condemns millions to starvation, war and unemployment. Production must be taken out of the hands of capital and controlled and planned by the freely associated producers themselves. This can be done, this socialist future can be achieved, only by those same producers, the class of wage-workers. The rule of capital and profit over human labour has to be overturned. Labour must be emancipated, by labour itself.

INTRODUCTION

THIS is the outlook on which a party of the working class must be based. It is when they are more and more coordinated and directed towards this aim that all the work and struggles of the working class and all those fighting against capitalist oppression and exploitation will achieve success.

If we look at the particular situation in which the working class finds itself today, we see that the separation of the working class's 'industrial wing' from politics has become even more obviously the opposite of what is in fact necessary. How ironic that the unions are to 'keep out of politics' when the state itself is by far the largest employer! How are workers in unions to defend 'non-politically' their interests without fighting against the ruling party and the state, when their employer is the state, or a state service, or a state-owned industry, or a local or regional branch of the state; or if privatisation of a state service or industry is proposed? How are they to defend their wages, conditions and jobs if they do not use their organised strength in a fight - a political fight - to get rid of the anti-union laws? And within the unions, is it not very clear that in order to fight the great banks and international companies who more and more dominate the world, trade unionists need international solidarity and organisation?[3] With such organisation and solidarity it would soon become apparent that the multinationals are not all-powerful, but because of the interconnections of their world-wide operations, are in fact very vulnerable to the coordinated actions of their workers.

But what do the existing big unions and international union confederations do about this? Nothing. If it had been left to them, the Liverpool dockers would have been left to fight alone, as the miners were in 1984-85. What is needed is precisely a political fight by trade unionists to remove these bureaucrats, integrated as they are into the capitalist system, and build a real international network capable of organising international solidarity.

That it what the Liverpool dockers have begun to do.

---
[3] Far from keeping out of politics, these banks and multinationals use governments to advance their work, as Shell uses the murderous dictatorship in Nigeria and the rubber companies that in Indonesia.

A new party, and the trade unions

THESE questions of trade unionism are therefore highly political. The trade union movement has everywhere to be reconstructed on new foundations, in such a way that it is adequate to facing the insoluble problems of the structural crisis of capitalism, continually intensified by today's global capital operations. These problems hit the working class in the form of privatisation, casualisation, mass unemployment and massive cuts in elementary welfare services. But these are part of an overall social crisis in which the younger generations are ruthlessly exploited and denied any future, the peoples of Asia, Africa and Latin America are virtually written off, and everywhere right-wing repressive regimes are prepared to replace what democratic rights exist.

The reconstruction of the trade unions as fighting organisations is taking place with inescapable political implications, at the centre of which is the reconstruction of working-class internationalism. The workers who organise in their unions to make them into such fighting organisations are engaging in the historic work of reconstructing the working-class movement after generations of class-collaboration and betrayal. The Labour (Socialist) and Communist Parties, each in their own ways, used their leadership and control of unions and international union federations to further their own accommodation to capitalism.

When workers now set about the reconstruction of internationalism in the trade union movement, they will need to organise themselves politically, in their own internationalist, socialist party, against the bureaucracy and its politics. A new party will be a party of the working class, those organised in unions and those not yet organised - not a party standing above and outside the working class and the unions.

Trade unionists are now beginning to go beyond the situation where for so long they have had to defend themselves against the employers' attacks and at the same time against their own bureaucratic leadership which disperses and separates them and helps the employers. They are beginning to take the initiative themselves, to work and organise as a workers' international as we have seen in the Liverpool dock strike. Once these forces come together to form their own party, a great change begins, not only in ideas but in practice. Such a party will not be controlling and manipulating the workers and unions from outside, but will lead the fight for internationalism and socialism *inside* the class movement of the working class.

The trade union bureaucrats say it is impossible to take action because there is a law against it. We say: we fight despite the law, as the miners and others have done. We fight against the law; laws can be changed, and we need a political movement to get rid of the anti-union laws. We shall build a mass movement to demand their repeal, against a Labour as well as a Tory Government.

For such a political struggle, a party of the working class is needed; strategy and united actions are needed. We cannot accept that such a vital struggle be left to workers separated, their efforts divided, in their individual unions.

Can 'Labourism' be revived?

THE battle to get rid of the anti-union laws is based on a principle we cannot let go: the independence of trade unions from the state. In the political struggle in the trade unions, and inscribed on the banner of a new party, we stand by this principle, along with the principle of internationalism.

Because these are principles, and not mere words, the fight to get rid of the anti-union laws, like the fight to build an international movement of working-class solidarity, cannot be held back because it would bring the working class into conflict with a Labour Government as well as a Tory one. In this conflict, political unity, a political party able to fight against the state forces and the government, Labour or Tory, is necessary. Understanding that in capitalism's structural crisis Labour has irrevocably broken from its 'reforming' role, and is part of the attacks which capitalism demands from its servants - it is from this principle that we must start. To entertain any hopes that Labour can be 'pressured' to return to a reforming role, and to restrict the movement of the working class to demands for pledges from the Labour Party at election time or in government, would today be a betrayal.

Even to suppose that it is possible to revive reformism, to create some kind of 'true Labour' or 'real Labour' party, able to win reform measures answering the needs of the working class, is a dangerous illusion. This is because since the early 1970s Britain and the world capitalist system have moved further and further into the structural crisis in which not reformism but the taking back of past reforms is what capitalism insistently requires as its method of dealing with the working class. In rebuilding its own class movement in the course of resisting these attacks, the working class will be enormously strengthened by the additional forces driven into struggle who previously thought they were in more secure and privileged positions.

To these must be added the many millions, especially young people, who are suffering from unemployment, homelessness and the absence of any prospects of a future. These millions know that Blair and 'new Labour' regard them not only as an embarrassment but as a threat to their image of protectors of the interests of respectable, narrow-minded and prejudiced 'Middle England' (hence Blair's 'we are the party of law and order'). And these millions know too that the trade unions as they are at present, controlled by bureaucracy, do absolutely nothing about the plight of the unemployed, the homeless and the youth.

A new working-class party worthy of the name, opening the door for the strength of the working class to come into politics, will have to be the champion of all these most oppressed and exploited people, giving them a new confidence and drawing their leaders into its ranks. The abstention and disillusionment of the mass of young people with politics will stop once they see a really fighting working-class movement. We can begin to see how a new party must be born in the midst of a broad mass movement, its programme representing the many and varied needs of that mass of people.

It will become obvious in practice, just as it is in theory, that the integration of the trade union bureaucracy into the capitalist state is one thing, but the integration of the working class is quite another! István Mészáros in his recent book B*eyond Capital* (1995) has shown in great detail how the failure of the traditional reformist parties is not something accidental, or the result only of individuals or groups like 'new realists', 'new Labour', and so on, but is rooted in 'the greatly reduced margin of manoeuvre of the capital system as it entered its structural crisis in the 1970s'. This necessitates a complete change in the working-class movement:

> The organisational forms and corresponding strategies for obtaining defensive gains for labour proved to be strictly temporary and in the longer run totally unviable. There was never any chance of instituting socialism by gradual reforms within the framework of the established mode of social metabolic reproduction. What created the illusion of moving in that direction was precisely the feasibility - and for a few decades also the practicability - of defensive gains, made possible by the relatively untroubled global expansionary phase of capital. Thus, not only there can be no room now for granting substantive gains to labour - let alone for a progressive expansion of a margin of strategic advancement, once foolishly but euphorically projected as the general adoption of the 'Swedish model', or as the 'conquest of the strategic heights of the mixed economy', etc. - but also many of the past concessions must be clawed back, both in economic terms and in the domain of legislation. This is why the 'Welfare State' is today not only in serious trouble but for all intents and purposes dead.' (*Beyond Capital*, p.240)

Mass unemployment, permanent and structural for an increasing proportion of the jobless (matched of course by Labour's abandonment of any pretence of a 'full employment' policy), is the sharpest expression of this change. It is important to see how this afflicts a wider and wider range of working people. In past times we were told that the large and most efficient companies, technologically advanced, were the best guarantee of our future. Now we can read: 'The big employers used to be the ones who provided secure, and often pensionable, employment, but they are the ones now cutting jobs. Meanwhile, the new jobs that are being created are in small firms and are mainly part-time, short-term contracts, freelance or self-employed.' And it should be noted that the British Government is now discussing removing the employment rights of those workers in small businesses employing less than 20 people - of which there are 10 million! The Government's own Labour Force Survey showed that of the small net increase in employment in the year ending autumn 1994, only one-eighth (13 per cent) was in permanent jobs. The rest were temporary (46 per cent) or self-employed (41 per cent). The so-called Jobseekers' Allowance will hit hard those who are classed as 'middle-income'. They have paid contributions entitling them to 12 months allowance, but will receive only six. Furthermore, as middle income earners, they are more likely than others to have some savings, which means they will not be eligible for income support. And since October 1995 there has been a cutback in income support for mortgage payers.

As background to these changes, it should not be forgotten that over one and a quarter million householders are in 'negative equity', that is, they owe more on their mortgages than the value of their houses. Over 250,000 mortgages are more than six months in arrears. The so-called 'Middle England' does not reach very far down any longer, and Blair's appeal will narrow, not broaden.

The recession of the early 1980s hit heavy and traditional industries like shipyards and steel, but that of the 1990s has been called 'classless'. Thousands of jobs in 'high-tech' enterprises, particularly in defence industries, have disappeared, as they have in retailing and distribution. Sackings by the big banks, already at a high level in 1995, will amount to

INTRODUCTION

20,000 in 1996. This pattern has meant that towns in the South have begun to suffer in the same way as did those in the North and the Midlands in earlier years. In calculating the basis which all this produces for a new and strong socialist movement, we can be sure that these trends are not temporary and insignificant, but permanent. After all the blather from Major about a classless society, and from generations of reformist-minded sociologists and economists, most of them backing the Labour Party, about 'we are all middle-class now', we can find that the Rowntree Inquiry on Income and Wealth concludes that distribution of income is more unequal in this country than at any time since 1945!

What is needed is not the pipe-dream of a revived Labour Party reformism, but a party with a socialist programme which addresses these needs.

2

National or International?

IT IS not by any means something new, to say that the party of the working class must be internationalist and international. There have been great international working-class parties in the past. Always, the rejection of internationalism has meant betrayal.

This is because the working class is an international class by its very nature. Capital stalks the world seeking out the commodity, labour-power, wherever it can be most cheaply bought and exploited. The only weapon of the working class against this is organisation, combination, solidarity. Therefore, when capital is able to turn worker against worker on the grounds of nationality, the working class of both nationalities is weakened.

It follows also that the working class of any country has common interests with the workers of all other countries, and not with the capitalists of its own country. Indeed it needs the working class of other countries in order to fight and win against its real enemy, its 'own' capitalist class. Any political or trade union leader who calls upon the working class to act or to fight in the 'national interest' is a traitor to the class. All the talk from the TUC and Labour leaders today about a 'partnership' with capital, in the 'national interest', all the Blair talk about 'making Britain great again', is the same treachery. Any Labour or trade union leader who gives the smallest concession to racist discrimination, or who refuses to defend the victims of racism, or who compromises even in the slightest with

20,000 in 1996. This pattern has meant that towns in the South have begun to suffer in the same way as did those in the North and the Midlands in earlier years. In calculating the basis which all this produces for a new and strong socialist movement, we can be sure that these trends are not temporary and insignificant, but permanent. After all the blather from Major about a classless society, and from generations of reformist-minded sociologists and economists, most of them backing the Labour Party, about 'we are all middle-class now', we can find that the Rowntree Inquiry on Income and Wealth concludes that distribution of income is more unequal in this country than at any time since 1945!

What is needed is not the pipe-dream of a revived Labour Party reformism, but a party with a socialist programme which addresses these needs.

2

National or International?

IT IS not by any means something new, to say that the party of the working class must be internationalist and international. There have been great international working-class parties in the past. Always, the rejection of internationalism has meant betrayal.

This is because the working class is an international class by its very nature. Capital stalks the world seeking out the commodity, labour-power, wherever it can be most cheaply bought and exploited. The only weapon of the working class against this is organisation, combination, solidarity. Therefore, when capital is able to turn worker against worker on the grounds of nationality, the working class of both nationalities is weakened.

It follows also that the working class of any country has common interests with the workers of all other countries, and not with the capitalists of its own country. Indeed it needs the working class of other countries in order to fight and win against its real enemy, its 'own' capitalist class. Any political or trade union leader who calls upon the working class to act or to fight in the 'national interest' is a traitor to the class. All the talk from the TUC and Labour leaders today about a 'partnership' with capital, in the 'national interest', all the Blair talk about 'making Britain great again', is the same treachery. Any Labour or trade union leader who gives the smallest concession to racist discrimination, or who refuses to defend the victims of racism, or who compromises even in the slightest with

Blair slavishly echoed all other capitalist spokesmen by saying that the collapse of the Stalinist regimes in the Soviet Union and Eastern Europe proved that planned economy and social ownership did not work, and that the future lay with a managed capitalism (managed by Labourites loyal to capitalism like himself, that is). In fact the collapse of Stalinism was part of the structural crisis of world capitalism. and not at all a collapse of socialism, which of course never existed in the Soviet Union. The whole relationship between imperialism and the Stalinist bureaucracy was in fact the main pillar of capitalism's system of 'managing'. The result was the very opposite of what Blair saw as a victory for capitalism.

This meant that in its structural crisis, a crisis deepened and not at all ameliorated by the collapse of Stalinism, the capital.ist class had to continue and intensify its attack on the conditions and rights of the working class. It had to do so in a situation where it inevitably provoked a heightening of the class struggle but was deprived of the main weapon (Stalinism) which had for so long blocked the development of a socialist, internationalist consciousness and organisation in the working class.

This working-class internationalism, the reconstruction of which is the essence of the work of all Marxists, revolutionary socialists, is the very opposite of what the remnants of the Stalinist bureaucracy and the Labourite (social-democratic) politicians and trade union leaders are doing. They bend their efforts to become part of a mythical 'new world order'. In fact this means only that they put themselves forward, each in their own way, as the best candidates for carrying out the necessary attacks on the working class.

This stark contrast between the needs and spontaneous development of the class movement of the working class on the one hand and on the other the class role of its traditional parties, now revealed to all in the new situation, is the objective content of the great possibilities today for building a world party of socialist revolution, with sections in every country. That will be the first step in the fulfilment of the programme of the Fourth International founded in 1938. When the reformists forward at the end of 1924, flew in the face of the Marxist understanding that socialism only becomes historically possible by surpassing the achievements of capitalist production and world market. Instead of this, Stalin's idea was the expression of the position and the interests of the bureaucracy which regulated the economy and state of the isolated and economically and culturally backward young Soviet Republic. In reality, the only future for the workers' state established by the Russian Revolution in 1917 was for new revolutions in the major capitalist countries, yet that prospect was sacrificed, and the struggles of the working class subordinated to the short-sighted interests of the bureaucracy in preventing capitalist intervention in the Soviet Union.

It cannot be repeated too often today that the time has arrived for a successful reconstruction of working-class internationalism, as the working class and all socialists are being forced to recognise that both these 'national' departures from socialism have totally failed the working class. A vital part of this development is that all those socialists who previously could not see any way to organise independently of reformism and Stalinism now confront a different political world. New organisations, new parties, regroupments bringing together forces previously separate and even antagonistic, must come about in response to new objective necessities - and new divisions too, where there is a failure to understand the demands of the new situation. For this new situation - a world situation favourable to the working class - the working class needs new, internationalist means of struggle.

After the spectacular collapse of the apparently mighty Stalinist bureaucracy at the end of the 1980s, the spokesmen of the ruling class had a lot to say about a 'new world order'. This phrase has no positive meaning whatsoever: there is no 'world order'. The only meaning we can attach to the phrase is that until the late 1980s such 'world order' as existed was managed only through the class compromise between capitalism and the Stalinist bureaucracy, which has now ceased to exist.

It was to be expected that social-democrats such as Tony

duty of sending millions of workers to their deaths in the trenches in defence of 'national democracy'. Throughout the century, the Labour Party, like all the European 'socialist' and 'social-democratic' parties, has remained servile to the capitalist class of its 'own' country.

Just as Labour leaders in time of war have always willingly helped to send countless thousands of working men to their deaths in defence of capitalism, so in peace-time Blair, like those before him, prepares to impose the terrible costs of capitalist crisis on the backs of the working class.

IT WAS because of the 'patriotic' treachery of the parties of the Socialist International in World War I that, inspired by the Russian Revolution which in 1917 overthrew the Tsarist autocracy, many workers in all countries joined the newly formed parties of the Communist International.

But after only a few years, under the pressure of imperialist armed intervention and economic isolation in backward conditions, the working class of Russia fell under the leadership of Stalin and his faction, representatives of the controlling bureaucracy. And this Stalinist leadership managed to win control of the Communist Parties of the rest of the world. These are not just dead historical facts. The history has vital lessons for us today.

The Stalinist parties of the Soviet Union and throughout the world have failed the working class, as has social-democracy. In the 1990s, the Stalinist parties have collapsed, and the Labour Party finally abandons even the pretence of being a working-class party - at the very point where the working class can and must have an internationalist strategy and programme against the burdens imposed by capitalism's structural crisis, and organise in an international party. And this historic failure derives from the abandonment of internationalism, equally by Stalinism as by Labourism.

For the whole Stalinist edifice was built upon the doctrine of 'socialism in a single country'. This doctrine and strategy, borrowed by Stalin from the old social-democracy and put immigration controls or restrictions on the right of asylum, is guilty of the same treachery.

Not only the nature and the existence of the working class in capitalism are international, but so are its aims, its future. Today's productivity of labour, higher beyond belief than anything in the past, harnessing science and technique and bringing into social interrelation the skills and effort of the peoples of the whole world, can be the basis of a society of abundance for all, yet it is turned against humanity itself.

For capital, productivity means productive of profit, to be accumulated into more capital. In this pursuit of profit, capital and those who personify it must be indifferent to the destruction of human beings, of culture, and of nature itself, which results. It is absolutely imperative, for the very future of humanity, that the power and technology now at the disposal of society (until now, of course, this means 'at the disposal of capital') are controlled, planned, restrained, subjected to the conscious and creative consideration and decisions of a free people.

It goes without saying that capital's mode of operation is the opposite of this social control. The socialism at which the working class and its party have to aim can therefore only be international. This is not the place to write a history of the working-class movement,[4] but this has to be said: 'Labourism' and Stalinism, it is now becoming generally recognised, have failed the working class in the twentieth century. At the very source of this failure was betrayal of working-class internationalism. The socialist or social-democratic parties built up in Europe in the last quarter of the last century, and the Labour Party, despite some very correct internationalist words in the resolutions of their 'Socialist International', very soon became 'national' parties, tied to the institutions of the capitalist state, restricting the struggles of their followers to national issues, and in World War I each collaborated enthusiastically with their 'own' capitalist class in the 'patriotic'

---

[4] We propose to deal in a separate publication with the historical questions involved in a reckoning with reformism and Stalinism.

and ex-Stalinists talk of a 'new world order' they are only telling us that they are in the dustbin of history. There is no new world order. There will be a new world party!

THIS prospect, it must be re-emphasised, does not arise only in the heads of socialist theorists who contemplate the new relationship of class forces and come to understand what is necessary. As Marx long ago posed it: does 'reality', i.e. the class movement of the working class, itself move towards what is theoretically necessary? The reconstruction of internationalism is a very material thing. In more ways than one, the working class in the struggles forced upon it by imperialism's crisis finds that these struggles take on an international character.

Two recent examples are outstanding. With the collapse of Stalinism and the 'old world order', Yugoslavia broke up. The corrupt caste of bureaucrats, led by Milosevic, in control of the state apparatus in Belgrade, capital of Serbia and of the former Yugoslavia, had for years moved towards a reactionary 'Greater Serbian' nationalism, persecuting the Albanians of Kossovo and asserting domination over the other nationalities in the Yugoslav state. Nourished and incited by this degeneration of the Serbian Stalinist leadership, and acting as its instrument, Karadzic and his right-wing nationalist Serb leadership living in Bosnia made war on the newly independent Bosnia-Herzegovina.

This war on behalf of 'Greater Serbian' nationalism aimed to smash the multi-ethnic nature (Bosnian-Croat-Serb) of the urban and rural communities in Bosnia. In a heroic war of resistance, the people of Bosnia defended that multi-ethnic unity. In doing so they were defending - against the thoroughly reactionary nationalism into which Stalinism had developed - what remained of the gains of the Yugoslav revolution during World War II. In defending the multi-ethnic nature of their communities they were and still are defending the unity of the working class, rejecting the division along lines of national origin or religious affiliation required by imperialism and its ex-Stalinist agents. It is a principle of the working-class movement to give unconditional support to this fight of the Bosnian people, as of any oppressed people, for the independence and integrity of their nation.

What is important here is that in defence of the Bosnian people's fight, the Workers International was able to initiate and carry through an international campaign in the working-class movement to bring support by working-class revolutionary means, material solidarity, going beyond just the affirmation in words of such support. Workers Aid for Bosnia, organising aid convoys to the working-class stronghold of Tuzla, has carried out this work for over three years, and has been able to bring in the support of trade unionists in western and eastern Europe. Of real and symbolic significance was that the first convoy went under the emblem 'From Timex to Tuzla!', starting as it did from the picket line of the Scottish workers against the Timex multinational corporation.

After years of stubborn defence, against Stalinism, of the aim of unity of the working class of eastern and western Europe, and defence of the principle of supporting the right of self-determination by revolutionary means, it has now been proved in practice, by the determined and extremely difficult fight of a relative handful of comrades, most of them young and even new to the workers' movement, that this new world situation is favourable to the working class, in that the Stalinist obstacle to internationalism in action can be overcome. It would be difficult to overestimate the magnitude of this change.

The second example, equally powerful, is the development of the Liverpool docks dispute, which began in September 1995. The dispute began over sackings, immediately behind which were the issues of casualisation, imposition of temporary contracts, the attack on full-time jobs, rights at work, and all those aspects of the employers' offensive which affect not only all dockers but millions upon millions of workers in Britain and in other countries. Speaking six months after the strike began, at one of the thousands of meetings addressed by the strikers' delegates up and down Britain and abroad, one docker summed up the experience of the shop stewards' committee: 'We started with a dispute; we became a vanguard'. It is true.

The significance of the leadership given by the dockers was summarised as follows in Workers Press of 16 March 1996: 'Workers Aid for Bosnia and the Liverpool docks dispute are two compelling instances of the new stage reached in the development of the working-class movement: the reconstruction of its internationalism, key to the reconstruction of the working-class movement itself and basis of the new party which must be built.'

3

Capitalism Yesterday and Today

WHEN at the end of the 1980s the Stalinist regimes in Eastern Europe and the Soviet Union collapsed, the capitalist media and political spokesmen all over the world could not restrain themselves: 'Socialism has failed', they told us, hailing the arrival of a 'new world order'. 'Capitalism and free enterprise have triumphed over communism.' 'Planning does not work, the market does'. Even many socialists predicted that the restoration of capitalism would now proceed apace in the ex-Stalinist countries, giving capitalism a new lease of life.

In reality, what followed the collapse was a new world disorder. To put it more accurately, the 'disorder' or historical crisis that fundamentally characterises imperialism (i.e. 20th-century capitalism) resurfaced in even more violent forms. The economic and political contradictions which make up this disorder had for a considerable time been displaced in the temporary 'order' established through World War II and the post-war coexistence with Stalinism. In the late 1960s and early 1970s this temporary and relative equilibrium already came under great pressure, unmistakable symptoms of which were the Vietnam War and its consequences, the civil rights movement in the United States, the 1968 general strike in France and uprising in Czechoslovakia, and the collapse of the Bretton Woods agreement and the 'gold and dollar standard' in 1971.

Then and throughout the subsequent period, while United States capitalism maintained its world dominance, it was more and more threatened by the rise of new and powerful competitors. At the same time, the failure of successive governments from Brezhnev to Gorbachev made it obvious that the Soviet economy and state structure were in terminal crisis. The crisis and then collapse of the Stalinist regimes and of the whole international Stalinist apparatus have undermined the whole international system of political, military and diplomatic relations.

But these relations were mechanisms through which international capital had been able not only to adjust to the consequences of the Russian Revolution and the overturns in eastern Europe and China but even to attenuate its own internal contradictions as a system. It was not simply that Western commercial, industrial and especially finance capital more and more penetrated the Soviet Union, Eastern Europe and China. The more important advantage gained by the ruling classes of the capitalist countries was in the first place political. This process began long ago. Ever since the Stalinist degeneration of the Soviet state and the international communist movement began in late 1924 under the false banner of 'socialism in a single country', the working class in one country after another had been betrayed and in effect controlled through the abandonment of revolutionary politics by the Stalinists. The communist opposition to Stalinism was physically wiped out in the Moscow frame-up trials and purges, culminating in the assassination of Trotsky in 1940.

At the end of World War II, the contribution of the Stalinist bureaucracy to capitalism's overcoming the threat of revolution in Europe and Japan was crucial. It can be briefly summarised.

The Soviet bureaucracy's peace agreements with the victorious Western powers (Yalta and Potsdam) were the public and open face of a political strategy which meant the rejection of socialist revolution and the disarming of the working class in all those countries where the Communist Parties had mass influence, in particular in Italy, France and Japan. The Yalta partition of Germany and Europe into capitalist and Soviet 'spheres of influence' was a mighty blow against any prospect of proletarian internationalist struggle. Within months the programme of 'peaceful, parliamentary roads to socialism' and 'peaceful coexistence with capitalism' was imposed on every Communist Party in the world. Without the conditions of relative 'social peace' ensured by these policies, the capitalist post-war recovery and new period of expansion would not have been possible.

A further advantage for the capitalist class was that this new period of expansion provided conditions in the advanced countries in which the old national reformism of the social-democratic and Labour Parties could maintain its existence. These parties had the added advantage that the crimes of the Stalinist bureaucracy discredited communism, with which capitalist propaganda was happy to confuse it.

The oppressed peoples of the colonial countries were caught in the same historical impasse. In dozens of countries in Africa, Asia and Latin America, millions of people died in heroic national-liberation struggles in the post-war period. But Stalinist parties, following faithfully the Soviet bureaucracy, dragged the working class behind its 'own' national bourgeoisie, preventing it from developing its own independent leadership and movement for socialism. The bureaucracy went further. In Namibia, South Africa and Angola the assistance given by the bureaucracy to the liberation movement included the arming of internal 'security' forces which systematically tortured and killed fighters who questioned the bourgeois leadership's strategy and tactics. In country after country this whole political line resulted in a repetition of the blood-bath inflicted on the Shanghai workers at the hands of the nationalists in 1927, which had been one of the first fruits of Stalinism.

But this is by no means all. When 'independence' came to these countries the Soviet bureaucracy gave economic and military support to the bourgeois regimes which came into power. Many of these were military dictatorships, brutally suppressing all working-class and democratic opposition. But the security and intelligence forces they used for this suppression were equipped, trained and advised by Soviet personnel. 'Socialism in one country' came to mean socialism in no other country. For the bureaucracy in the Kremlin, the search for 'allies' to maintain an economic, military, and diplomatic coexistence and balance with imperialism was paramount.

Leaders and spokesmen of the imperialist powers may often have bewailed the fact that the Soviet Union in those years exerted great influence on the newly independent countries. The reality was that this state of international 'rivalry' was of incalculable advantage to imperialism, compared to the consequences for them if the national-liberation struggles had developed into working-class revolutions.

The enormous benefit gained by international capitalism from these Stalinist policies of accommodation, through which the working class was controlled, was by no means confined to the years of expanded capitalist reproduction, between the end of World War II and the early 1970s, when Keynesian policies of inflationary stimulation of the economy and 'full employment' were possible in the major capitalist countries. A further great advantage to the ruling class was that when the capitalist crisis required a change to all-out offensive against the working class - euphemistically called 'neo-liberalism' and consisting of policies personified in Thatcher and Reagan - that attack could be launched under conditions still favourable to the attackers, because the Stalinist and social-democratic leaderships retained their hold on the working class until the end of the 1980s.

We have seen that there were fundamental causes for the offensive in all the major capitalist countries against established working-class conditions and past gains such as the 'welfare state'. Capitalism could no longer put off or 'displace' its historical contradictions.

> What we are witnessing today is a two-pronged attack on the class of labour not only in the 'underdeveloped' parts of the world but, with dangerous implications for the continued viability of the established mode of social metabolic reproduction, also in the capitalistically advanced countries. We witness: (1) in all fields of activity a chronically growing unemployment, even if it is often camouflaged as 'flexible

labour practices' - a cynical euphemism for the deliberate policy for the fragmentation and casualisation of the labour force and for the maximal manageable exploitation of part-time labour; and (2) a significant reduction in the standard of living of that part of the working population which is needed by the operational requirements of the productive system in full-time occupations.[5]

This reverses a trend which basically had begun even before World War II. The economic crash of 1929 and the Great Depression of the 1930s had seemed to many socialists, and even non-socialists, to be a 'final crisis', a collapse of capitalism from which successful struggles for socialism must emerge. While it is certainly true that in one country after another social and political crises produced pre-revolutionary and revolutionary situations, the fact is that the revolutionary opportunities were lost (Germany 1919-23, Italy 1919-21) and then, after the rise of the Stalinist bureaucracy, betrayed (China 1925-27, the British General Strike of 1926, Germany 1933, Spain 1936-39). Against this background, imperialism was able to contain its crisis for a relatively long period.

By no means was this done in some 'peaceful', non-contradictory way. Roosevelt's New Deal and the revival of the US economy through Keynesian policies after the Great Depression was possible for the now dominant imperialist power. In Germany, Italy, Spain and Japan only fascist repression, crushing of the working-class movement, and the war drive to redivide the world could serve as the form of capitalist rule. Fascism, totally unprecedented massive destruction, ending with the nuclear holocaust, military expenditure and post-war reconstruction: this was the price humanity had to pay for capitalism being able to enter a new and temporary phase of expansion. Rosa Luxemburg's historical alternative, 'socialism or barbarism' was being acted out even then.

Throughout this period, the dominance of US capital was

---

[5] Meszaros, *Beyond Capital*.

completed. The decline of Britain and France had already been evident after World War I. In World War II and the years following, there came the elimination of all the remaining advantages of Empire, traditional financial services and protected markets of the old powers. US capital, with the banks in the lead, now operated without these old barriers, dominating not only through the fast-growing multinational corporations but also through its control of the international financial institutions - World Bank, International Monetary Fund, etc. - and the financing of the European capitalist powers' post-war 'recovery'.

THE whole post-war period was therefore marked by this fully developed global dominance of US capital - a new relationship of US imperialism to the older powers and, no less important, to the countries which had previously been colonies or dependencies of those older powers. On this basis US imperialism 'led the free world' in gratefully accepting the Soviet bureaucracy's political, economic and military adjustment to world capitalism. It was this new totality for imperialism, emerging after World War II and temporarily displacing its structural contradictions, that constituted the 'world order' which, already under great strain, definitively broke up when the Stalinist bureaucracy collapsed in 1989-90.

There is no 'new world order' to replace it. This is because none of the above factors which made possible the earlier displacing of the fundamental contradictions can be brought back to life. Capitalism must turn in on itself, and that is indeed the process that began with the anti-union laws and the whole offensive against the 'welfare state' led by politicians like Thatcher and Reagan. That the Stalinist bureaucracy collapsed before this offensive could be completed and its gains consolidated in new forms of rule was truly a boon for the international working class. The working class now fights back without the burden of Stalinism.

Despite being deprived of the advantage of Stalinist influence and control over large sections of the working-class movement, particularly its leading elements, capitalism cannot pull back from going through with its offensive. Each capitalist, whether in the form of a giant multinational corporation or an independent business, is increasingly driven to impose harsher conditions upon labour; and each capitalist nation-state is similarly forced by competition for markets to resort to political repression to discipline the workforce on behalf of the ruling class. This it must do despite the fact that it inevitably arouses working-class resistance and conflict which feeds into and threatens to give focus to what is already a crisis of 'law and order', crisis of domination and social control, collapse of traditional values visible to everyone.

This has important implications for the kind of programme which a socialist party must have in the present situation. The Labour Party in Britain's recent sharp turn to the right directly reflects these needs of capital, and this is why Blair's attack on Clause Four has brought forward among wider circles the question of the need for a new party. As well as abandoning Clause Four, 'new Labour' proposes savage attacks on the state benefits of people deemed to be 'work-shy', at the same time abandoning the policy of full employment. It drops the principle of universal entitlement to pensions and other benefits. It opens the door to 'private enterprise' in education and health-care. In the name of a 'new welfare state' and 'stake-holder economy' it drops the welfare state. It wants to be the party of law and order. Blair pledges to businessmen in Japan and Australia that he will not repeal the anti-union laws so that Britain will be 'safe' for their investments. He has instituted a dictatorial rule of 'the leader' inside the Labour Party. Was the class nature of the Labour leadership ever clearer?

We have entered a period, then, in which capitalism has no more room to expand. Though consistently ignored by economists, this is a real truth of the so-called globalisation. The system has run out of options. The enormous growth in productivity of labour, resulting from the last half-century's advances in science and technique, imperiously demands a method of social control by the direct producers in free mutual association, planning their long-term relationship with the resources of nature instead of plundering them mercilessly and dangerously as does capital in the search for profit, and allowing ample free time for all for cultural development for all. Against this necessity, capital demands that all production, distribution and consumption and all human culture be subordinated to the freedom of capital to exploit labour. This means repressive political restrictions, attacks on democratic rights, and strengthening of that legitimised monopoly of violence called the state. These are the very opposite of what humanity at this stage of its development requires.

CONTRAST this with the days of early capitalism and the industrial revolution. There were countless social evils; there was mass poverty; there was denial of rights. In fighting against these evils, socialists were compelled at the same time to acknowledge that the capitalist system, based on the exploitation of propertyless wage-labour, was the contradictory path through which the productive basis for socialism and freedom would develop. Capitalism was taking forward mankind's productive forces. It is precisely because capitalism can no longer develop those forces, but destroys them, even endangering humanity's survival, that the fight for socialism today can be successful.

István Mészáros writes:

> As we know, in Marx's lifetime the capital system was far from subsuming under its own reproductive framework every country on the planet. Thus it was still very far from its stage of development where the destructive dissipation of natural resources and social wealth had to become an objective condition of capital's expanded reproduction. Likewise, the development of the instruments of destruction was still very far from the point where it could directly threaten human life everywhere, in sharp contrast to our own perilous conditions of existence . . . we had to wait for the occupation and reproductive domination of every little corner of the world by the major capitalist powers, leading to the conflagration of two World Wars, before the

destructive implications of capital's uncontrollability could be fully sized up in their massive materiality. And we have by no means reached the end of this process. For the much talked about 'globalisation' - assuming the form of an apparently irresistible integration of the productive and exchange processes of the capital system in the entire world - foreshadows new antagonisms and potential destruction.[6]

By the end of the nineteenth century, capitalism entered a new stage, that of imperialism. The concentration and centralisation of capital and accordingly the massive scale and complex interconnectedness of production and commerce were the only possible form that could be taken by the socialisation of production. Industrial and finance capital merged. New capitalist powers had come on the scene to challenge Britain's world supremacy. These imperialist powers were the political and military instruments of the monopolies, ready to fight wars for the division and redivision of a world now dominated by the conflict between monopolies for markets and for the best conditions for the export of capital.

In the major capitalist (imperialist) countries a 'labour aristocracy' grew up on the basis of the super-profits of imperialism and found political expression in the opportunist, social-chauvinist wing of social-democracy. There opened up the epoch of wars and revolutions. Lenin described this imperialist era as the highest, last stage of capitalism, that is to say, the stage of capitalism in which proletarian revolutions and the transition to socialism would begin.

A mere couple of decades after the beginning of the imperialist period, Marxists had seen the explosion of imperialism's contradictions in the first great imperialist war (1914-18). The enormous social and political crises produced by that war brought revolutionary situations in a number of countries. But the war itself had also brought to a head the opportunist tendency in the social-democratic parties, as the great majority of them gave support to their 'own' bourgeoisie

---

[6] Mészáros, *Beyond Capital*

as soon as the war began. The consequent revolutionary struggles found these social-democrats on the side of counter-revolution, as in the bloody suppression of the German revolution.

Only in Russia was there a successful socialist revolution. The economic conditions for building socialism did not exist in that country. Imperialism had broken 'at its weakest link'. The Bolsheviks knew that the future of the Russian revolution depended on holding on to power until 'the workers of the advanced countries come to our aid'. Of course no one could have predicted this course of events. It was not possible, before 1914, even to discern the depth of the anti-internationalist degeneration in the Second International, let alone prepare effectively to defeat it in time. Only in the course of the struggle itself could it become known that the Russian Revolution would indeed remain isolated, and that this isolation would in a short time make possible the consolidation of a Stalinist bureaucracy which then through its policies itself perpetuated that very isolation and soon became counter-revolutionary.

Similarly, a correct historical perspective on the epoch allowed no one to know in advance that US imperialism could strongly assert its superiority, clearing from its path - especially in World War II and the subsequent 'peace' - the inherited advantages of the older powers with their empires, thus not only adjusting to the rule and expansion of the Soviet bureaucracy but profiting from it economically as well as politically. This US superiority and its relationship to the Soviet Union made possible not only the massive stimulus to capitalist economy by 30 years of state-underwritten production of weapons of mass destruction, an industry which became the motor of unprecedented technical innovation. There were of course contradictions within these mechanisms themselves. For example, the enforced rivalry in military build-up and scientific research and development placed eventually unbearable burdens on the Soviet economy. The permanent, international character of the socialist revolution, determined by the inherently insoluble contradictions of the capitalist mode of production in its imperialist stage, was historically confirmed in these developments, as later in all others, but it was confirmed negatively, so to speak. Trotsky was to characterise the whole period as one in which the objective conditions for socialist revolution were overripe, so that the crisis of humanity was concentrated in the crisis of working-class revolutionary leadership.

This is an example of how the dependence of the political, legal and ideological superstructure on the economic base must be understood always as a relationship within an interacting totality, and of how this general formula should not be a substitute for concrete analysis. On the political ground prepared by the betrayals of social-democracy, the confinement of the revolution to the 'weakest link', and the usurpation of Soviet power and world Communist leadership by the Stalinist bureaucracy, and despite enormous inter-imperialist conflicts, new revolutions, unprecedented economic crises and the biggest war in history, imperialism was able to effect a series of adjustments and 'displacements' of its historic contradictions over the whole period between the post-1917 revolutionary wave and the fall of the Stalinist bureaucracy in 1989-90.

For this period of some 70 years capitalism could put off or postpone what we must now expect and prepare for: the unfolding of its historic, structural contradictions in a continuous series of revolutionary situations. With the collapse of Stalinism and the manifestation of the accumulated basic structural contradictions of the whole system, this unfolding can be postponed no longer. In the struggles that lie ahead, the working class will reconstruct itself and develop adequate Marxist leadership.

4

Towards the Socialist Offensive

WHAT lies in front, then, is not a sudden general collapse or universal revolutionary explosion, but a series of uninterrupted struggles, made inevitable by the removal of capitalism's options for postponing its structural crisis. Even though there will be temporary setbacks and short-lived compromises, these struggles have no solution within capitalism: already we have the examples of the miners' strike in Britain in 1984-85 and the 1992-93 closure of pits. In and through these struggles it is essential to fight for that reconstruction of the working-class movement which is the indispensable preparation for the pre-revolutionary and revolutionary crises which will arise.

This fight means that in every one of the partial struggles - *in* them, not advising from outside and definitely not 'from above' - a socialist, Marxist perspective must be developed. Capitalism does not disappear from the scene under the weight of its internal contradictions. As Marx showed many years ago, there is a struggle of classes in which 'men become conscious of the contradictions and fight them out'.

In the 20th-century agony of capitalism's structural crisis and its prolongation through the events explained above, the conflict between capital's unquenchable thirst for accumulation of value, on the one hand, and the necessity of a society of free and cultured individuals consciously regulating the relations between them and with nature, on the other, has produced a universal social and cultural crisis. All the traditional values, ideologies and institutions of social control are breaking up. The break-up is there for all to see in the crises of the family, of education, of the institutions of 'law and order', and in a hundred other ways. These inseparably linked crises pose problems which will have to be addressed by a socialist strategy, which cannot be restricted to 'economic' demands if it is to be able to unite the forces for socialist revolution.

The anti-union laws, the large-scale state violence used in the 1984-85 miners' strike, the Criminal Justice Act and prison reforms in Britain, the many instances of persecution amounting to state racism, and the repressive restrictions and deportations flowing from new immigration controls and the Asylum and Immigration Bills; these are only the beginnings of the capitalist class's turn to direct political repressive measures as its options of reform through social compromise finally run out. There is no 'reform' answer to this inevitably intensifying offensive of the ruling class. And in any case, as we have seen, the 'reformers' and liberals, advocates of 'partnership' and 'social contract', are openly abandoning even the pretence of fighting for reforms, and advertise their credentials as 'the party of government', of 'law and order'. The defensive institutions and organisations which could to a certain extent deliver the goods to at least sections of the working class in the advanced capitalist countries can no longer do so. They have a future only as bureaucracies incorporated into the capitalist state, or in the case of the unions, as transformed organisations capable of mobilising the working class for the necessary socialist offensive. Here lies the importance of overcoming once and for all the division between the so-called industrial and political arms of the working-class movement.

The socialist perspective, as we have seen in Chapter 2, cannot but be international and internationalist. All attempts to restrict working-class politics to some narrow national, parliamentary, reformist framework are dangerous. They express the pressure of a milieu of middle-class activists, careerists, publicists and so on trapped in the framework of 'official' politics, sceptical about - because afraid to face - the prospect of a working-class movement reconstructed on internationalist, revolutionary lines. These elements, even those who speak in the most 'left' terms, are about to be caught between the twin pressures of, on one side, a Labour government using the repressive power of the state against all working-class opposition and, on the other, the working class itself. That situation will produce centrist tendencies of various kinds. Some will move to the left, some to the right, and the way revolutionaries orientate towards them will be important. But waiting is fatal. Today - that is, before all this happens - it is obligatory for Marxists to take the initiative in bringing together the elements of a new, socialist party.

This is true especially because there will be millions of workers, not yet drawn actively into politics, who will vote Labour in the hope of some improvement in the conditions inflicted on them by the Tories but will be quickly disillusioned. Then the question of the need for a new party to represent their interests will confront millions in real experience. What is now a debate will become a great social movement. An ounce of political and theoretical preparation now will prove then to be immeasurably valuable.

PARTY AND PROGRAMME

IT IS not difficult to see that the collapse of Stalinism inevitably aggravates capitalism's crisis and, most important, deprives the capitalist class of its main instrument for controlling the working class and preventing it from developing in every struggle its revolutionary potential.

But there is another side to this, a side which is not always understood, as is shown by the question, 'Why emphasise that Trotskyism is not only anti-Stalinism?' This new situation faces us as Marxists with new tasks, theoretical and political. Capitalism in this latest phase of its historical crisis faces heightened contradictions, its parasitic features more and more predominate, and the conflict between globalisation/socialisation of production and the nation state intensifies. The ruling class needs to impose harsher and changed forms of exploitation, which require the destruction of rights won by the workers in the past. This must provoke class struggles which lead either to new, more repressive forms of rule, under which the necessary discipline can be imposed, or to revolution.

We have concluded that in these battles the situation is favourable for the working class and thus for the forces rebuilding the Fourth International. Because it is a new situation, it requires us to tackle new theoretical, political and organisational tasks. The political and theoretical work of the last three-quarters of a century has centred on the struggle against Stalinism, as the force which imposed the crisis of revolutionary leadership, in which humanity's crisis was concentrated. The control established by Stalinism meant that Marxists, Trotskyists, had to swim against the stream.

The question of building the indispensable revolutionary leadership is now posed differently; Stalinism is dead. When Marxists confront the new theoretical and political tasks, they do so as part of the necessary process of learning to swim with the stream! We now must face directly, in practice as well as in theory, the great questions of actual leadership, strategy and tactics from which we were for decades sealed off by the isolation which Stalinism could impose on the Fourth International.

alteration of men on a mass scale.'

The utopian socialists could not get beyond the ideas of the bourgeois Enlightenment when they confronted this question. For them, a section of society standing above the common mass would have to change the masses through education. Marx showed that the working class must transform itself; in the struggle forced upon it by capitalism. Forced to struggle to change circumstances, it would in the course of that struggle transform itself. The proletariat's own revolution was the secret of its casting off its oppressed character and taking the first great step towards true humanity. When we try to grasp the fight on reforms and partial demands as essential to the revolutionary struggle of the working class, as we must, then we have to be with the working class in fighting, against the degrading effects of capitalism in decay, to preserve and develop its unity and integrity as that force which makes the socialist revolution.

Programme and strategy in the political preparation for the 'new party' must have as their content not only a set of demands and a demonstration of their relation to the socialist objective. Again: the 'mass communist consciousness' which Marx knew was necessary for the socialist revolution was, as he insisted, arrived at only by the working class itself achieving 'the alteration of men on a mass scale'. This 'alteration is not a matter of enlightenment, education, but rather of how the working class changes itself through the struggles, at first defensive, forced upon it by its relation to capital.

Our fight for the development of a programme and strategy in the new situation has to be firmly based on these conquests of Marxist theory, as was Trotsky's in the *Transitional Programme*:

If capitalism is incapable of satisfying the demands inevitably arising from the calamities generated by itself, then let it perish. 'Realisability' or 'unrealisability' is in the given instance a question of the relationship of forces, which can be decided only by the struggle. By means of this struggle (N.B.), no matter what its immediate practical successes may be, the workers will come to understand the necessity of liquidating capitalism.

conditions of unemployed people, especially youth; the starvation, disease and homelessness suffered by millions in Africa and Asia; and the destruction of basic human rights in all corners of the planet - how all these great problems derive from the same structural crisis of capitalism and have no solution except a common struggle for socialism.

All such issues and demands must be incorporated into the programme of a socialist party. And what must always be at the front of our minds is that no longer can any of these issues be taken on board by capitalism in the new phase of its structural crisis. The more a socialist party uses its influence and organises its members to assure for each of these movements the maximum strength, support and success - instead of indulging in the time-worn and always false method of 'intervening' in such struggles for propaganda and recruiting purposes - the stronger a genuine mass, pluralist movement for socialism will grow and the more a socialist party will establish strong and principled relations with that mass movement.

The role of a party whose objective is socialism and the overthrow of the power of capital must be to show the way for the working class to build, in and through its initially defensive struggles, the understanding and confidence, the organisations and everything else that will be necessary to win the decisive struggles in front.

Lessons from history can help us to see more clearly what this means today. First, an example. Here is an extract from a resolution of the International Workingmen's Association in 1866, entitled 'Juvenile and Children's Labour (Both Sexes)':

> It may be desirable to begin elementary school instruction before the age of 9 years; but we deal here only with the most indispensable antidotes against the tendencies of a social system which degrades the working man into a mere instrument for the accumulation of capital, and transforms parents by their necessities into slave-holders, sellers of their own children. The right of children and juvenile persons must be vindicated. They are unable to act for themselves. It is, therefore, the duty of society to act on their behalf. If the middle and higher classes

neglect their duties toward their offspring, it is their own fault. Sharing the privileges of these classes, the child is condemned to suffer from their prejudices.

The case of the working class stands quite different. The working man is no free agent. In too many cases, he is even too ignorant to understand the true interest of his child, or the normal conditions of human development. However, the more enlightened part of the working class understands that the future of its class, and, therefore, of mankind, altogether depends upon the formation of the rising working generation. They know that, before everything else, the children and juvenile workers must be saved from the crushing effects of the present system. This can only be effected by converting social reason into social force, and, under the given circumstances, there exists no other method of doing so, than through general laws, enforced by the power of the state. In enforcing such laws, the working class do not fortify governmental power. On the contrary, they transform that power, now used against them, into their own agency. They effect by a general act what they would vainly attempt by a multitude of isolated individual efforts.

This resolution, the significance of which for today surely speaks for itself, was drafted by Karl Marx. If the defence of the rights of children, underlined by Marx, against the degradation imposed by capital was indispensable in 1866, how much more so is it today?

IT WAS on these lines that the Workers International made the following statement in 1994.

RWANDA

Statement by the International Secretariat of the Workers International (to rebuild the Fourth International)

As we write the death rate amongst Rwandan refugees from cholera and other diseases is one person a minute. The sick are climbing under their mats to die so that others can wrap their bodies more easily, and the dead are lying so closely packed by the side of the road that tyre marks are visible where vehicles have been forced to drive over them.

We have to add to the whole crisis of authority and ideology, of all the institutions and values upon which the capitalist class has been able to rely in the past, a general crisis felt in one way or another by everyone, a sense of lack of direction of society, an angry and frustrated feeling that nothing is being done to replace the lost security and certainties of the past, whatever their limitations, a knowledge that those in power use that power only for their own purposes, a mistrust of all those who claim to be working for the national interest or the common good.

For this crisis of consciousness to have a positive political expression requires that there is a truly anti-capitalist and socialist direction and leadership for the struggles into which working people are forced. It is to that challenge that the orientation for a new party is the response. Here we are forced back to the question of programme, now from the aspect of how, on what strategic and tactical basis, the mass movement will develop in and through the partial struggles; how the defensive struggles against the new attacks of capital will be turned to the necessary offensive.

2. This question, of the relation of partial and defensive struggles of the working class to the necessary unified struggle of the class as a class for its own political power, for socialism, is of course not new. Nonetheless, the understanding and solution of this whole complex of problems has to start from the basis of the historical stage now reached by the whole in which they originate and which they continuously constitute. The fact is that the stage reached by capitalism's structural, global crisis today - a stage which began in the early 1970s with the end of the post-war expansion - is of a scope and depth which did not exist before. And this changes the relations between defensive struggles and the preparation of the revolution, between reform and revolution, because the conditions of options available to capitalism, in particular the options of controlling the working class through the Stalinist bureaucracy and in the advanced capitalist countries through reformist party and trade union

PARTY AND PROGRAMME 59

conditions of life and assumed security of existence of these millions it is at the same time breaking up the social base of social-democracy, and at the very time when it begins to become obvious to everyone that social-democracy not only can no longer guarantee any reforms but must play its part in removing past gains. The crisis of social-democracy thus goes far deeper than the wholesale corruption in the European socialist parties or the latent seething disillusionment with Blair.

The sociologists of the 1960s and 1970s could hardly have been more wrong. In the surface facts of the boom they saw a permanent 'modernisation', in which the 'underdeveloped' countries need only await 'take-off'. In the advanced countries' near-full employment and wage increases of those years they saw only the growth of a 'white-collar middle class', an 'embourgeoisement' of the working class, and something called a 'post-industrial society.' That the fundamental class relations remained unaltered and that the contradictions of capitalism accumulated under the surface escaped their notice, since Marx was, after all, out-of-date.

What has actually resulted is the very opposite of the trends they thought they discerned. The 'new middle class' is being brought sharply to the recognition that capital requires that its conditions of life and security must be the same as those proletarians with blue collars. (The sociologists, far from critically examining their past 'mistakes', now want only to bore us with their world-weary blather about 'post-modernism'.)

In saying that the developments of the last few years undermine the base of social-democracy - and at a time when there is no Stalinism to shore it up or to offer an alternative - the most important consideration is that these changes create the conditions for a working-class movement of great scope. The actual conditions into which millions of working people are forced lay the basis for a reconstruction of the organised working-class movement, its unions and parties, in which the traditionally more militant sections of the working class are joined on basic issues by millions who feel themselves thrust down into a loss of security and deprivation of rights.

Let us call on the workers of every country to move their organisations to make these demands on their governments. In South Africa, for example, let the COSATU unions tell the 'Government of National Unity', Mandela and De Klerk, to commandeer whatever is necessary from Anglo-American, De Beers and the rest. The workers of South Africa will respond to such a call, as everybody knows.

In Britain, France, Belgium, Germany, the US, the ruling classes of these countries have built their vast wealth from the brutal exploitation of Africa, from the slave trade to the diamond mines and uranium. It is this exploitation and oppression of half a millenium, and not 'inter-tribal conflict', that has kept Africa economically backward and has starved to death or butchered millions in Somalia, Ethiopia, Algeria and Rwanda, just as they did in Vietnam, Malaysia, Cambodia and in every corner of the world.

MARX fought against the socialist sectarians who dismissed or criticised trade union and economic struggles and struggles to get legislated reforms such as the eight-hour day and universal elementary education. On the latter, he was not concerned only with the fact that, as he explained, in forcing a legislated concession the workers would feel their concentrated political strength as a class. And though Rosa Luxemburg explains very well in *Reform and Revolution* that in and through trade union and parliamentary struggles what the workers learn is the need for a struggle for power, nor is this the whole story (even if she was absolutely correct to stress this side of it against Bernstein).

Marx understood very well that capitalism did not only concentrate and discipline the working class; part of the working class's struggle to equip itself for the socialist revolution was to organise to defend itself against the degradation and depravity imposed by capitalist exploitation. That was how Marx saw the struggle for the shorter working day. That was how, for example, he saw the struggle of the working class to defend the rights of children.

When we discuss programme today, then, should we not ask ourselves: if it was necessary to see the relation between reform and revolution in these terms in the 19th century (when capitalism was still developing the productive forces) surely it is at least as necessary today to have a programme of defence against every manifestation of the degradation and depravity inflicted on the working class by capitalism in decay? In the *Transitional Programme* Trotsky writes, in the section on the sliding scale of wages and hours: 'The question is not one of a "normal" collision between opposing material interests. The ques tion is one of guarding the proletariat from decay, demoralisation and ruin. The question is one of life or death of the only creative and progressive class, and by that token of the future of mankind.' And, explaining the nature of a transitional programme: 'In so far as the old, partial, "minimal" demands of the masses clash with the destructive and degrading tendencies of decadent capitalism and - this occurs at each step - the Fourth International advances a system of transitional demands.'

Most of the issues on which struggles develop and in relation to which the new party must be consciously fought for can be brought together under such headings: casualisation of labour, atomisation of the workforce, the consequences of 'deregulation', health, education, public services, protection of the old, racism, Bosnia, ecology; drugs, AIDS, closures, unemployment and destruction of communities, housing, 'inner cities', privatisation, democratic rights and powers of state. There are two 'dimensions' of all these issues which are of first importance in understanding their revolutionary implications: first, they tend, in our day, to immediately take on an international character, and second, the role of the state and the struggle against the state is central to all of them.

It is necessary here to return to basic questions of Marxist theory. The threat of barbarism posed by capitalism in decay forces us to return to the old question faced by Marx: If the men in our society are the products of their capitalist environment, how can it be that they will bring about socialism? He knew that the mass 'communist consciousness' necessary for this would come about not through 'education' carried out by enlightened individuals, but only through what he called 'the alteration of men on a mass scale'.

The utopian socialists could not get beyond the ideas of the bourgeois Enlightenment when they confronted this question. For them, a section of society standing above the common mass would have to change the masses through education. Marx showed that the working class must transform itself, in the struggle forced upon it by capitalism. Forced to struggle to change circumstances, it would in the course of that struggle transform itself. The proletariat's own revolution was the secret of its casting off its oppressed character and taking the first great step towards true humanity. When we try to grasp the fight on reforms and partial demands as essential to the revolutionary struggle of the working class, as we must, then we have to be with the working class in fighting, against the degrading effects of capitalism in decay, to preserve and develop its unity and integrity as that force which makes the socialist revolution.

Programme and strategy in the political preparation for the 'new party' must have as their content not only a set of demands and a demonstration of their relation to the socialist objective. Again: the 'mass communist consciousness' which Marx knew was necessary for the socialist revolution was, as he insisted, arrived at only by the working class itself achieving 'the alteration of men on a mass scale'. This 'alteration' is not a matter of enlightenment, education, but rather of how the working class changes itself through the struggles, at first defensive, forced upon it by its relation to capital.

Our fight for the development of a programme and strategy in the new situation has to be firmly based on these conquests of Marxist theory, as was Trotsky's in the *Transitional Programme*:

> If capitalism is incapable of satisfying the demands inevitably arising from the calamities generated by itself, then let it perish. 'Realisability' or 'unrealisability' is in the given instance a question of the relationship of forces, which can be decided only by the struggle. By means of this struggle (N.B.), no matter what its immediate practical successes may be, the workers will come to understand the necessity of liquidating capitalism.

PARTY AND PROGRAMME

IT IS not difficult to see that the collapse of Stalinism inevitably aggravates capitalism's crisis and, most important, deprives the capitalist class of its main instrument for controlling the working class and preventing it from developing in every struggle its revolutionary potential.

But there is another side to this, a side which is not always understood, as is shown by the question, 'Why emphasise that Trotskyism is not only anti-Stalinism?' This new situation faces us as Marxists with new tasks, theoretical and political. Capitalism in this latest phase of its historical crisis faces heightened contradictions, its parasitic features more and more predominate, and the conflict between globalisation/ socialisation of production and the nation state intensifies. The ruling class needs to impose harsher and changed forms of exploitation, which require the destruction of rights won by the workers in the past. This must provoke class struggles which lead either to new, more repressive forms of rule, under which the necessary discipline can be imposed, or to revolution.

We have concluded that in these battles the situation is favourable for the working class and thus for the forces rebuilding the Fourth International. Because it is a new situation, it requires us to tackle new theoretical, political and organisational tasks. The political and theoretical work of the last three-quarters of a century has centred on the struggle against Stalinism, as the force which imposed the crisis of revolutionary leadership, in which humanity's crisis was concentrated. The control established by Stalinism meant that Marxists, Trotskyists, had to swim against the stream.

The question of building the indispensable revolutionary leadership is now posed differently; Stalinism is dead. When Marxists confront the new theoretical and political tasks, they do so as part of the necessary process of learning to swim with the stream! We now must face directly, in practice as well as in theory, the great questions of actual leadership, strategy and tactics from which we were for decades sealed off by the isolation which Stalinism could impose on the Fourth International.

The possibility of developing Marxism is immeasurably increased, because there now exist qualitatively new and favourable conditions for the development of theory as a guide to practice.

It is in this sense that it has been necessary to emphasise that Trotskyism is not only anti-Stalinism. The failure to understand this manifests itself, characteristically, in a persistence of the habit of discussing political and historical questions independently of any theoretical-conceptual considerations. This had its dangers, even when the movement was inevitably preoccupied with the struggle to understand and expose the counter-revolutionary nature and role of Stalinism (see Trotsky's *In Defence of Marxism*), but such a laziness (to put it mildly) in matters of theory would now be fatal.

IN developing the indispensable discussion on programme for the new party, there are two sets of considerations.

1. The development of the crisis of capitalism in this latest phase brings rapid and far-reaching changes in social life, extremely important in the conditions of work (or non-work) of the working population but by no means restricted to these. To speak of only an 'economic' crisis is dangerously one-sided, notwithstanding that the whole social and cultural crisis derives from the historical contradictions of the capitalist mode of production. There is a thoroughgoing and insoluble crisis in the whole system of domination, the whole political, legal and ideological superstructure which the capitalist class, like every ruling class, requires. This crisis is reflected powerfully in a general malaise, frustration, rejection of discipline, and loss of any confidence in the old institutions of control, or in a secure and settled future.

Of great importance, and requiring the elaboration of a comprehensive defensive programme (defence which in order to succeed in any measure would have to become attack - another way of saying that it is a programme of transitional demands, in

Trotsky's sense, that needs to be elaborated), is the whole development over the last few years of great changes in the rights and conditions of employed workers, from the anti-strike and anti-union laws in Britain and other countries to the consequent drive to casual, part-time work, 'home'-work and individual contracts, removal of protection by national agreements, 'flexible' working times, longer hours and so on.

'Deregulation' and privatisation, mergers and take-overs, and the introduction of cost-accounting and the 'internal market' in services, all intensify these changes. There is a return of the most brutal forms of exploitation of women, children and youth.

We need urgent work on all these issues, and the elaboration of a programme of demands and resistance.

Politically, it is especially important that these changes are so socially wide-ranging. They affect the working population from university lecturers and researchers, schoolteachers, bank officers, and civil servants to workers in construction, manufacturing and transport. They affect the young, the middle-aged and the old. Thus millions of people are having their lives transformed according to the needs of big capital in its structural, historical crisis (structural and historical, i.e. not merely conjunctural: the unemployed men and women of today are not a 'reserve army of unemployed' who when the business cycle recovers will find work, but are in large numbers condemned to permanent unemployment).

And this is happening to millions of working people who in past decades had found the kind of jobs, income and security which many of them thought had lifted them out of the ranks of the working class. With their relatively privileged existence and conservative consciousness, they tended, in Britain and other advanced capitalist (imperialist) countries, to be assimilated into the labour aristocracy of skilled and better-paid workers. Together they formed the social base of the social-democracy which for so long has succeeded in subordinating the working class politically to its 'own' imperialism through parliamentary reformism.

As capitalism in its latest phase turns to brutally disrupt the conditions of life and assumed security of existence of these millions it is at the same time breaking up the social base of social-democracy, and at the very time when it begins to become obvious to everyone that social-democracy not only can no longer guarantee any reforms but must play its part in removing past gains. The crisis of social-democracy thus goes far deeper than the wholesale corruption in the European socialist parties or the latent seething disillusionment with Blair.

The sociologists of the 1960s and 1970s could hardly have been more wrong. In the surface facts of the boom they saw a permanent 'modernisation', in which the 'underdeveloped' countries need only await 'take-off'. In the advanced countries' near-full employment and wage increases of those years they saw only the growth of a 'white-collar middle class', an 'embourgeoisement' of the working class, and something called a 'post-industrial society.' That the fundamental class relations remained unaltered and that the contradictions of capitalism accumulated under the surface escaped their notice, since Marx was, after all, out-of-date.

What has actually resulted is the very opposite of the trends they thought they discerned! The 'new middle class' is being brought sharply to the recognition that capital requires that its conditions of life and security must be the same as those proletarians with blue collars. (The sociologists, far from critically examining their past 'mistakes', now want only to bore us with their world-weary blather about 'post-modernism'.)

In saying that the developments of the last few years undermine the base of social-democracy - and at a time when there is no Stalinism to shore it up or to offer an alternative - the most important consideration is that these changes create the conditions for a working-class movement of great scope. The actual conditions into which millions of working people are forced lay the basis for a reconstruction of the organised working-class movement, its unions and parties, in which the traditionally more militant sections of the working class are joined on basic issues by millions who feel themselves thrust down into a loss of security and deprivation of rights.

We have to add to the economic changes the whole crisis of authority and ideology, of all the institutions and values upon which the capitalist class has been able to rely in the past, a general crisis felt in one way or another by everyone, a sense of lack of direction of society, an angry and frustrated feeling that nothing is being done to replace the lost security and certainties of the past, whatever their limitations, a knowledge that those in power use that power only for their own purposes, a mistrust of all those who claim to be working for the national interest or the common good.

For this crisis of consciousness to have a positive political expression requires that there is a truly anti-capitalist and socialist direction and leadership for the struggles into which working people are forced. It is to that challenge that the orientation for a new party is the response. Here we are forced back to the question of programme, now from the aspect of how, on what strategic and tactical basis, the mass movement will develop in and through the partial struggles; how the defensive struggles against the new attacks of capital will be turned to the necessary offensive.

2. This question, of the relation of partial and defensive struggles of the working class to the necessary unified struggle of the class as a class for its own political power, for socialism, is of course not new. Nonetheless, the understanding and solution of this whole complex of problems has to start from the basis of the historical stage now reached by the whole in which they originate and which they continuously constitute. The fact is that the stage reached by capitalism's structural, global crisis today - a stage which began in the early 1970s with the end of the post-war expansion - is of a scope and depth which did not exist before. And this changes the relations between defensive struggles and the preparation of the revolution, between reform and revolution, because the conditions of options available to capitalism, in particular the options of controlling the working class through the Stalinist bureaucracy and in the advanced capitalist countries through reformist party and trade union

leadership, no longer exist!

There will be many proposals for new reformist and parliamentary parties in response to the disappearance of the 'Communist' Parties and the open abandonment of any working-class character by the social-democratic and Labour Parties. Such proposals (e.g. Arthur Scargill's Socialist Labour Party) will fail, and quickly, because they ignore this profound historical change. Behind the present political crisis in the working-class movement lies not a plot by right-wingers, careerists and middle-class agents, which can be defeated by restoring the reformist nature of the old parties or by forming new ones on the old lines, but the fact that for deep historical reasons social-democracy, as well as Stalinism, is finished.

The historical conditions for social-democracy - originally, the availability of 'superprofits' in the advanced countries for the conditioning and control of the working class, and then the ability of imperialism to find ways of overcoming its conjunctural crises and displacing its contradictions - are gone. The options are exhausted. It is no longer possible to rule through those 'bourgeois workers' parties.' Add to this not only the crisis and breakdown of all traditional ideological and legal methods of social control, the definitive collapse of Stalinism, capitalism's main and only other political resource, and you have the constituent elements of the unitary economic and political global crisis of imperialism.

It is on this basis that programme and strategy must be developed.

6

Programme and Party

IT would be a mistake to think that the great questions of capitalism's global and historical crisis which are the subject-matter of earlier chapters, can in some way be separated from the way a programme of transitional demands is to be elaborated.

It is essential that the programme of a new party be discussed and worked on in the immediate future with the participation of all those who are coming forward as the vanguard of the class in its struggles.

In this discussion, it will be necessary, for example, to prepare demands in the struggle against mass unemployment. This will be difficult, because we are no longer talking only about the reserve army of labour which always existed under capitalism, and which grew in times of cyclical crisis. Furthermore, the 'new jobs' which capitalist politicians shout about from time to time are mostly only temporary contracts and part-time jobs without any trade union-protected rights at work. The great multinationals decide their policies and plans on an international scale. Big business depends more and more on contracts, subsidies and policy decisions decided directly by the state. So it is impossible to fight unemployment by placing demands on single employers or even on the employers in a particular industry.

How can a programme to deal with the fight against unemployment and sackings be worked out, then, without starting from the international structural crisis of the system?

At the very least, the demand 'Open the Books!' directed at big business must be raised also against the banks, given today's greatly increased comprehensive domination of finance-capital. The same demand, 'Open the Books!', must be raised against the government itself.

If it is said that a programme of public works on a vast scale is financially impossible, then open the books! Let us have public inspection and control of the Exchequer! Let us have workers' control of the contracting and planning of public works!

If it is said that the state can no longer afford to pay the existing level of unemployment benefit because of 'shortage of money', then we have to say: there is no shortage of money; there is more money than ever before in history! Open the books of the state and its institutions as well as of big business. There are enough statisticians and economists sympathetic to the cause of the working class to overcome the 'creative accounting' of the hirelings of big business and the Exchequer.

For the working-class movement in Britain and other major capitalist countries to raise this demand can be a big step forward in creating the necessary solidarity with the masses in the ex-colonial countries. These millions carry the burden of permanent and increasing indebtedness to the banks of the United States, western Europe and Japan. They themselves have raised the demand 'Open the Books!' in relation to the plunder of their resources by big business. It was raised, for example, by the Workers Revolutionary Party in the Namibian elections of 1995. It is of the greatest importance that within the imperialist countries the banks and the governments are challenged on their exploitation through debt and investment in the 'underdeveloped' world. This could be a first step to the elaboration of an international plan of action against big capital, and a real contribution to the rebuilding of internationalism in the metropolitan countries.

Only in a socialist perspective can a programme of demands of this kind have any real meaning, because, like the innumerable demands now being made in response to capital's blind destructiveness, they cannot be realised outside of a socialist re-ordering of society. And that cannot be imposed from above but can only come about by the conscious self-action, in unity, of all these initially separate movements. Behind this necessity of socialism is the more and more unavoidable truth: that every single aspect of human existence, from individual health-care to the consequences of the destruction of the ozone layer, is today caught up in the uncontrolled, and by its nature uncontrollable, devouring of every resource, including humankind, by capital in search of the accumulation of more capital.

This uncontrolled and inhuman drive conflicts at every point with the need for a new system in which the associated producers make planned use - precisely with responsibility for the future, with control and restraint - of the wonderful conquests of science and technique.

It is this necessity of socialism that in principle unites the myriad issues and demands on which people all over the world come into conflict with the depredations of capital. That is why there are no individual solutions, or even sectional or national ones, to these problems in their totality. There is only a socialist solution. And that solution can be found only through the self-action of the class of labour, the force on which capital depends and in whose hands humanity's future rests. This is the basis of a socialist programme.

The abolition of capitalist private property in the means of production is at the centre of a socialist programme. But here again it is essential to lay the emphasis on the basic conception of socialism as the achievement of the emancipation of the working class by the working class itself. This means fighting for the utmost clarity about *who* abolishes capitalist private property, and about *who* actually 'owns' and controls the expropriated means of production. 'State ownership' of the means of production, distribution and exchange cannot be part of the transition to socialism unless certain questions are answered, certain conditions fulfilled; and this must be clear in the programme from the start.

FIRST: just what 'state' are we talking about? Transition to socialism means that the state, the instrument of oppression of the subject classes by the class in power, already begins to wither away. After the overthrow of the capitalist class, the working class itself has to smash up the old state and rule through its workers' councils. This transitional and entirely new form of state is necessary to deal with the opposition of the old ruling class inside and outside the particular country. It also must be the working class itself mobilised to reorganise production and all necessary social institutions. 'State ownership' in which the state apparatus is separate from and superior to the working class has nothing to do with a transition to socialism.

Nationalisation of an industry which is not imposed by a mass movement of the working class, which is not directed at weakening and eliminating the power of capital in the rest of the economy, which is controlled not by workers and consumers, but by a state apparatus which still serves capital, is not socialism or part of any transition to socialism. Such were the nationalisations carried out by the Labour Government in Britain in 1945-50. They were to the great advantage of capital in that they enabled national resources to be used to recapitalise and modernise run-down industries, which were later returned to private ownership. They functioned as cheap suppliers to private capital. They were bureaucratically run, against the interests of the workers and the consumers. And in the end they rewarded the workforce with massive closures, sackings . . . and privatisation!

So when we insist that the programme of a socialist party must define socialist nationalisation as part of the self-emancipation of the working class, we shall find that this coincides with the way the working class had already had to learn bitter lessons from its experience at the hands of the Labour Party and Labour governments.

Nor should it be forgotten that the working class knows very well what happened to nationalisation in the Soviet Union and

Eastern Europe. Planning and state ownership in a state where power was usurped by a bureaucracy, excluding the working class from control at any level, was part and parcel of a totalitarian tyranny, which at the same time made its own adjustment to world capitalism. The revolution of October 1917 and the dispossession of the Russian ruling class could have formed the basis for a transition to socialism if the relatively backward Soviet economy had not been isolated (see Chapter 2 above). But on the basis of that isolation, the Stalinist bureaucracy was able to defeat all opposition for a long period. Because of that bureaucratic domination, the outcome of Soviet economic and political development proved to be the process of restoration of capitalism, which the bureaucracy itself leads.

The lesson is clear. Without a development of the working class itself on the road to its own power, no reforms, nationalisations, or any other gains can be lasting. On the contrary, the contradictions of capitalism reassert themselves with ever-greater explosiveness. A socialist revolution is not only a political overthrow. The working class in such a revolution is not merely a mass force which provides the strength to break the capitalist resistance. It is the class which takes over the task of transforming society as a whole. Its role is neither simply political nor simply economic (productive); it has as its object not this or that reform, but its own self-transformation and with it that of the social order built on its labour. In changing society, men change themselves. The working class has to put an end to the whole historical epoch in which, as the direct producers, they have become from the standpoint of capital, mere objects.

Marx expressed this in many passages in his *Capital*:

> Capital is dead labour, that, vampire-like, only lives by sucking living labour, and lives the more, the more labour it sucks. The time during which the labourer works, is the time during which the capitalist consumes the labour-power he has purchased of him.

> Every kind of capitalist production, in so far as it is not only a

labour-process, but also a process of creating surplus-value, has this in common, that it is not the workman that employs the instruments of labour, but the instruments of labour that employ the workman ... the objective conditions of labour do not appear as subsumed under the worker; rather, he appears as subsumed under them. CAPITAL EMPLOYS LABOUR. Even this relation in its simplicity is a personification of things and a reification of persons.

Capitalist production is not merely the production of commodities, it is essentially the production of surplus-value. The labourer produces, not for himself, but for capital ... That labourer alone is productive, who produces surplus-value for the capitalist, and thus works for the self-expansion of capital. It cannot be otherwise in a mode of production in which the labourer exists to satisfy the needs of self-expansion of existing values, instead of, on the contrary, material wealth existing to satisfy the needs of development on the part of the labourer.

In overthrowing the power of the capitalist class, the working class completes the stage of achieving the class-consciousness necessary to win power; and then begins the task of using the power it has conquered to build the new society, abolishing itself as a class, reversing the relation between 'dead labour' or accumulated wealth and human labour. This task cannot be handed over to bureaucrats or commissars. It cannot be achieved even by the working class devoting itself to the reconstruction of the economy while its parliamentary representatives govern society as a whole. New institutions, workers' councils responsible for all the functions of society at all levels, are the necessary form of socialist construction as well as of working-class revolution.

A socialist programme has to say that; a socialist party working for the support of the working class has to give a clear answer to the question: where are we going? This means that in raising the urgent question of a new party, it is absolutely inadequate to simply make a criticism of the existing parties of the working class, however severe and deserved, together with a list of radical demands and a statement of the eventual aim of socialism. The call for a new party must be linked with all its consequences for the working class, all the consequences of reconstituting its class movement in the capitalist crisis of today, in every partial struggle building the preparations for the decisive battles in which it will achieve its self-emancipation.

7

What Kind of Party?

THE analysis of today's structural crisis of capital; the opening created by Stalinism's disintegration for working-class resistance to the consequences of that crisis; the plain fact that Labourism (social-democracy) has also failed the working class and now prepares to lead the capitalist attack on past working-class gains; the great fighting capacity shown by the working class internationally, exemplified in a succession of struggles in Britain from the miners' strike of l984-85 to the dockers' dispute and the battles fought by low-paid workers today: all these tell us that a new party of the working class must be not a reformist or parliamentary party, nor some kind of party conceived as a half-way house to possible future party for socialist revolution.

Those socialists who have already concluded that the Labour and Communist Parties must be replaced by a new party have to go beyond just a pragmatic conclusion that somehow a party with policies more radical than Labour, returning to the Labour Party's abandoned constitution and programme, will suffice. It is necessary to break with the whole idea of providing a party and programme 'for' the working class - an idea which of course fits perfectly well with a purely parliamentary strategy and with a division between the 'political and industrial arms of the movement'. If there is no such break, then all the sins of social-democracy will be repeated, and this time completely out of season, because there is no scope for reforms. Reforms, and parliamentary democracy itself, are certain to come under fierce attack from capital as it becomes clear that every avenue out of capital's structural crisis is a dead end.

Preparing for the formation of a new party, therefore, means the long and hard fight for a party that really *is* new. History shows that only the self-action of the working class can ensure lasting gains, that its battles can be won not as things in themselves but only in a socialist, revolutionary perspective and as part of a developing strategy for socialism. History tells us therefore that a new party can be founded only as one made up of those who come forward as the vanguard of that class. If it is not founded out of these very struggles, it will be an abortion. There is no social force that can win socialism except the social force that is forged in these battles: the working class learning from struggle, increasingly united behind its own vanguard.

In 1996, as we near the end of a long period of Tory government, the working class faces the prospect of a 'new Labour' government led by Blair. The frustrations accumulated through years of ruling-class offensive inevitably express themselves in a surge of expectations, a general aspiration for change, a hope that Labour can change things. Millions of people who vote Labour - and who until now have been assured that there is no political role for them as workers except to vote in the hope of a new government - will be rapidly disillusioned. When they press for their expectations to be fulfilled, they will meet the force of the state, mobilised by a government of the party which has commanded the allegiance of the vast majority of the working class for nearly a century.

A new party can be built in and through the mass movements which this historic shock will produce. And for these struggles we must prepare with the utmost urgency. Those who can be united now in this understanding have to *organise as Marxists, preparing now and in the months to come not only the programme but also the network of organisation and contacts which constitute the new party's real relation with the class.*

This means concentrating on Marxist theoretical work on the new questions which face the working class. It means bringing together around a common political newspaper, a newspaper which serves as organiser, all those who share the perspective of a new party built out of the developing movement of the class. And it means the widest possible organised discussion throughout the workers' movement, and among intellectuals, students, and fighters on all social and community issues, on the central question of preparing for the fight against the Tory government and the future Labour government, and the foundation of the new party. This is how socialists need to work now, rather than making a sectarian proclamation of a new party prematurely cut off from the vital experience of struggle now being prepared for masses of people.

Central to this preparatory work in the next few months is organised political activity in the trade unions. The Liverpool dockers' struggle has shown decisively that the reconstruction of the class movement of the working class is a political reconstruction. By their success in taking their fight into the international arena - even organising at short notice two international conferences of dockers' delegates from 15 countries - and by sustaining their fight despite the anti-union laws, the dockers have shown the way forward to millions of workers who face the same problems which started the dispute: casualisation, destruction of jobs.

The fatal division between the movement's 'industrial' and 'political' arms can be overcome. In 1990 the International Trade Union Solidarity Campaign (initiated by the Workers International) was set up along these very lines. Its three principles - independence of trade unions from the state; internationalism; workers' democracy - embody the necessity of a political solution to the crisis in the trade unions brought about by the increasing integration of the trade union bureaucracy into the capitalist state. The building of such a political alliance between workers in all trade unions is a goal that goes far beyond the old 'left factions' and 'broad lefts' within particular unions, and is one of the most important elements in the building of a new party.

Every form of activity in preparation for a new party should be guided by the aim of bringing into existence a party that is bound up with every section of the working-class movement; has connections and working relations with all associations and groupings of the labour movement; recruits members from all these sections and is able to unite their efforts; attracting to its ranks all those who come to the front in the struggles of their fellow workers and who see the need to unite all these struggles as the struggle of the whole class.

Such a party will have a truly working-class character, but it will not be confined to workers. It will not succeed in its aims if it does not also attract intellectuals, students and all those who come to the fore in the fight to defend communities or to stop big business and the state from destroying the environment and trampling on human rights. This will be a party which fights for the working-class movement to take up the cause of the most oppressed and exploited, including the unemployed and the oppressed peoples of the so-called 'underdeveloped countries'. It will embrace workers of all national origins.

Such a party must reflect therefore, in its programme, structure and composition, the changing composition, changing problems and changing needs of the working class, which we have outlined in earlier chapters. There is no doubt that the universality and depth of capitalism's structural crisis are deeply affecting layers of society which for decades had seen their future as safe within capitalism, providing a support for the politics of class compromise. Now many of them are subjected to the same attacks which afflict the 'blue-collar' workers. Millions of young people are bitterly alienated from the capitalist order. People not of the working class are drawn into opposition on a wide range of issues.

The struggles which will erupt on an even wider scale once the disillusionment with a Labour government sets in will surely take the form of a broad social movement, in which strike actions, though centrally important, will not be the only form of action. Such a movement was already foreshadowed in the 1968 and 1995 events in France, and in the mobilisations against the Stalinist bureaucracy in eastern Europe. As the political reconstruction of the working-class movement develops, with the building of a new party at its centre, it will take responsibility for encouraging and assisting all these elements of the movement, and we shall see emerging in these broad social struggles a 'workers' councils' form of development. This is the ultimate aim of the fight to overcome the 'industrial/political' division. These are the organs of class struggle which will become the focus of a power which confronts the enemy class, and its state, as a class.

Because the new party must have no aim other than the historical objective of the working class itself, its self-emancipation, it must combine maximum openness and democracy with maximum power of self-discipline, the ability to unite and centralise its efforts.

What does this combination of democracy and centralism mean? It means that it must be at the centre of the working class's efforts to free itself of the bureaucratic control imposed on it by the Labour and trade union leaders throughout the century and by Stalinism since the 1920s. United, disciplined action cannot come from a discipline imposed from above, but only from a mutual understanding of what is to be done, and from the ability of those leaders who are entrusted with authority to win the confidence of those who elected them. Such a leadership, with such a relationship to the ranks, comes only from the test of experience. It cannot and must not be taken on trust. The real content of centralisation of the work of a party and of the working class is not primarily a matter of organisational rules, even though constitutional safeguards are essential. As has been stressed throughout this pamphlet, what is most important is that programme, strategy and tactics are soundly based on an objective understanding of the relations between the classes, the stage reached by imperialism's crisis, and the lessons of our history.

For this Marxists must wage a constant fight to develop this understanding. They must study not only the experience of the working class but also the totality of the relations between and within all the classes, as the basis for winning new forces and uniting the actions of the working class. This work is the 'centre' of centralisation. The organised activity throughout the working-class movement of a party based on this work aims to give the maximum force to the spontaneous resistance of the working class, and to inspire - and learn from - the embryonic socialist consciousness which develops in struggle.

8

The 'New Party' and the WRP

WHAT is the relationship of the Workers International (to Rebuild the Fourth International) to this understanding of the necessity of a new party?

This is at first sight something of a conundrum. The Workers Revolutionary Party is surely already a party, is it not? Have not the Trotskyists known and said for more than 60 years that what the working class needs is a new party ('the fight for alternative revolutionary leadership')? What then does it mean to call for a new party now?

The answer is, in essence, what we have tried to explain in the preceding pages: that the disintegration of Stalinism and the maturing of the structural crisis of capitalism, now beginning to bring home to the working class in experience the bankruptcy of reformism, make inevitable a succession of struggles in which it is not only a tiny minority who realise the need for a new party. So we must pass, from the long and necessary period in which Marxists were for the most part restricted to explaining the need for a new party and exposing false leaderships, to the period of immersing ourselves in the struggles through which a new party can be formed. In recent years, especially since the miners' strike and then in trying to comprehend the collapse of Stalinism and its massive implications, our own movement (now the Workers International) was compelled to clarify some basic questions, often through sharp clashes, even crises and splits. And, with the benefit of hindsight given by our present tasks and today's struggles, we believe this clarification was truly necessary – which does not mean that it is a finished process.

In the first place, the WRP in Britain had to put an end to a long course of development in which the clique gathered around G. Healy consistently pursued opportunist politics and descended to degenerate bureaucratic abuses of their authority. In 1985 this clique was expelled. The first lesson we had to learn was that the split we decided to make was itself one manifestation of the long-drawn-out crisis of the Fourth International as a whole.

When we look back at 1985 we can see that the degeneration was the result of the failure to resist the pressure of Stalinism over a long period, culminating in opportunist adaptation, for example, to bourgeois-nationalist leaders whose own politics could only flourish in the international relation of forces made possible by the Stalinist bureaucracy's 'understanding' with imperialism. Instead of working for independent working-class leadership in the national-liberation struggles, confident in the fact that the crisis of the Stalinist bureaucracy would end in its overthrow or collapse, the WRP under Healy's leadership adapted to the national bourgeois leaders, in effect capitulating to the idea that the existing world relation of class forces, sustained by a powerful Stalinist bureaucracy, was more or less permanent.

In finding a road back to working-class internationalism, and in trying to understand what it meant to say that at stake was overcoming the crisis of the Fourth International, the principal question that faced us was the nature of Stalinism. At the root of every major revision and split in the history of the Fourth International had been the false notion that Stalinism had a 'dual nature': on the one hand counter-revolutionary, bourgeois, on the other proletarian, revolutionary. The struggle to clarify the counter-revolutionary nature of Stalinism is well documented. It was not only a matter of understanding our own past. In the present context what is important is that without this clarification it would have been impossible to comprehend the depth and scope of the qualitative change marked by the then imminent collapse of Stalinism. So, when that collapse came, there could have been no basic understanding of the new period and the new responsibilities of leadership in the 1990s.

We then very soon had the opportunity to learn the same lesson, on the nature of Stalinism and the implications of its disintegration, in a very compelling way. Comrades in the Workers Revolutionary Party of Namibia had made contact with us just before the first elections following the country's independence. They took a firm stand against the nationalist movement SWAPO, now standing as a party and poised to win a two-thirds majority in the new Assembly. Our Namibian comrades led a fight to expose the atrocities which had been perpetrated by the SWAPO security forces during the armed struggle for national liberation. Systematic torture, incarceration in underground dungeons, and executions, had been inflicted, not on traitors and collaborators but on SWAPO's own fighters, members of the SWAPO Youth League, who had dared to challenge politically the line and methods of the bourgeois-nationalist leadership. Comrades returning from SWAPO's prison camps played a large part in the campaign of the Namibian WRP and its allies.

The shocking truth was becoming clear. The state terrorism of the Stalinist regime in the Soviet Union - organised through the Moscow Trials and the internal and international work of the NKVD and KGB, and used to liquidate countless thousands of workers and intellectuals suspected of opposing the bureaucracy - had been 'exported' to the 'national-liberation movements' and the governments they formed after formal independence. Then as now those who opposed Stalinism and bourgeois nationalism with working-class internationalism were condemned as 'enemies of the people'[8]. It was clear that the assistance given by the Soviet state to the armed struggle in the colonial countries was accompanied by 'assistance' of another kind: security training and personnel, backed by political indoctrination, which tied the Communist Parties within organisations such as SWAPO or the ANC to bourgeois-

---

[8] And then as now it was necessary to counter decisively those who advocated remaining silent on this counter-revolutionary activity of Stalinism because it might give aid and comfort to the forces of imperialism against the Soviet Union or against the national-liberation movements.

THE 'NEW PARTY' AND THE WRP

nationalist politics and armed them with the material force to suppress opposition from the left. In this way the Soviet bureaucracy thought to make the outcome of the liberation struggles strictly subordinate to the international balance necessary for its own permanent coexistence with imperialism.

We were soon to discover that the South African Communist Party and African National Congress had played the same role in South Africa, exemplified and exposed in the murder of the young Stompie Moketsi and others by the 'necklacing' gangs of Winnie Mandela's ANC security forces, and by the brutal suppression of ANC mutineers. In 1995, when the Workers International began discussions and mutual work with the African Liberation Support Campaign in London, we found comrades who had well understood that 'left-wing' organisations and governments raised and supported by the Stalinist bureaucracy were in fact the most efficient instruments for ensuring the continued rule of imperialism and suppressing the popular forces. To the examples of Namibia and South Africa were now added identical stories, graphically documented, from Angola and Mozambique.

In these events, the whole theoretical fight to clarify the nature of Stalinism as counter-revolutionary found itself marching together with the unmistakable and indelible experiences of thousands of fighters in the great mass movements in Africa[9]. It has been very well said that the reconstruction of the working-class movement cannot be completed without 'a definitive reckoning with Stalinism'. We believe that the arduous struggle to which we refer above, to overcome the revisionist notion of a 'dual nature of Stalinism', will be seen as an essential preparation for that reckoning. On this basis we in the British WRP came more and more to see the primary importance of international work, to which we devoted all our resources. We participated in the work of the Preparatory Committee for the Reconstruction of the Fourth International. At that time we failed to come to agreement on

---

[9] Again, all these experiences were published, and we shall republish them in collected form, with the main documents on the supposed 'dual nature of Stalinism', to supplement this pamphlet.

the next steps with the International Workers League (LIT), at that time based in Argentina (but later, in 1995, a Liaison Committee was formed between the LIT and the WI). We came to the conclusion that the reconstruction of the Fourth International was above all an inseparable part of the necessary reconstruction of the working-class movement as a whole.

In Budapest in 1990 the Workers International was formed. One of its first steps was to initiate the International Trade Union Solidarity Campaign. A section of the Workers International was formed in the former Soviet Union. Open work became possible in eastern Europe, and as part of the WI the League of Hungarian Revolutionary Socialists was formed. A section was formed in South Africa. In 1993, in face of the war and 'ethnic cleansing' conducted by the Greater Serbian nationalist and ex-Stalinist regime in Belgrade against the independence and unity of the people of Bosnia, it was our Serbian comrades who proposed the organisation of convoys to Tuzla in international proletarian solidarity.

In 1992-93, the mass movement in support of the miners against the hundreds of pit closures made it crystal-clear that a turn in the situation in Britain was taking place. Not only did hundreds of thousands come on the streets, but support and solidarity groups sprang up in many places, recalling the support groups of 1984-85. In these support groups and in conferences called by the Community and Union Action Campaign (CUAC), many people active in working-class and community struggles discussed the need to unite their struggles. We considered that the mass support for the miners, no matter how successful the TUC leadership might eventually be in diverting and dissipating it, emerged because millions could see in the attack on the miners the shape of their own future fate and future struggles. Whatever the ebbs and flows, it had to be understood that the crisis behind this embryonic consciousness would not go away but would intensify, and that the wave which surged forward in late 1992 would return. There was building up a mass anti-government feeling which would soon result in a Labour government and a confrontation between the needs of the working class and the rapidly rightward-moving social-democracy. And in this new political situation the role of Stalinism in misleading past struggles, including the miners' strike of 1984-85, could not be repeated.

Having begun to understand that reconstruction of working-class internationalism (including reconstruction of the Fourth International) means not merely a 'regroupment' of existing Marxist organisations, but a reconstruction of the working-class movement, we now had to go a step further. We had to address the question: now that the working class must reconstruct its class movement, and can do so without the burden of the Stalinist bureaucracy, what does this mean in terms of the working class building its own party? How will this process relate to our own need to overcome the relatively isolated and largely propagandist character of our past?

We began to recognise, at first slowly, that however crucial and correct our insistence on the crisis of leadership, we had now to learn afresh that the decisiveness of revolutionary leadership does not mean that the spontaneous revolutionism of the working class, its 'socialist consciousness in embryonic form', should be at all underestimated. Quite the contrary: it is this very spontaneous revolutionism that demands the highest level of theoretical work and understanding, the maximum level of work in the working-class movement by Marxists. Just as 'the emancipation of the working class is the task of the working class itself', so the reconstruction of the working-class movement is the task of the working class itself! Our work for a revolutionary party must take place within that reconstruction, not 'from the outside'.

We were reminded of Lenin's words to Russian socialists: 'The strength of the present-day movement lies in the awakening of the masses ... and its weakness lies in the lack of consciousness and initiative among the revolutionary leaders'. And we were reminded of Trotsky's words: 'With the rise of a movement, the task of Marxists consists in, supported by the wave, bringing in the necessary clarity of thought and method.'

Along this path we came to understand that if a party is to be formed able to lead the class in the struggle for socialism it cannot be a group putting itself forward to the class as its 'vanguard party'. It must be, rather, the vanguard of the working class forming itself into a party. In other words, it cannot be a party 'supplied' to the working class, but a party *of* the working class, constantly building from that vanguard.

# 9

THE NEXT STEPS

ON March 16 the conference called in London by Workers Press to discuss 'The Crisis in the Labour Movement and the need for a new Socialist Party' carried the following resolution:

This conference resolves that the working class needs a new party for socialism. Now the task is to take the discussion on the programme, the organisation and the formation of a new party as widely as possible into the working class. We affirm that it must be a party OF the working class, formed out of its struggles, and not a party 'supplied' to the working class. Conference constitutes a steering committee, open to all present and all who share this common objective. The next tasks are:

● to organise in every area a report meeting on this conference;

● to participate actively in the main struggle of the day, building a network of support committees for the dockers. This network can be the basis of permanent working-class organisation to support such struggles.

The discussion in every area should firstly centre on how to unite the working class on the problems confronting the dockers, and at the centre of this need for unity is the urgent need for a socialist party. Out of the dockers' fight must come the bringing together of the vanguard of the working class in one party.

We will seek every avenue of discussion and united action with members of the SLP and discussion and participation with the Socialist Alliances in various areas.

> The steering committee should work to set up a 'policy research unit' to assist in all struggles.
>
> Conference resolves to reconvene in October this year to discuss the next step.

Why is it said, in this resolution, that it is in and through the movement built up in support of the dockers' dispute that the vital question of the new party is now decisively raised?

First, because solidarity with other workers in struggle is an elementary principle which it is essential to reassert, as the working class reconstructs its class movement. Second, the kind of solidarity which grew up in the miners' support committees has to be continued, and, this time, not allowed to subside, so that there begins to be constructed a permanent network growing stronger with every stage of the struggle. This means that, in the build-up of support for the dockers and then for others who take the brunt of the fight, we do not only find the best forum for discussing the need for the new party, we are actually putting together the links and the modes of action which will make up that new party.

But third, and most important, the dockers' fight (and this will be true of all the struggles now coming up) has come about on issues which not just dockers but the working class as a whole now must take up.

Everywhere the employers are trying to impose conditions where union organisation is broken up, permanent jobs eliminated, and casualisation in various forms introduced. It becomes impossible to earn a living wage without working inhumanly long hours, and in many cases without being on call at all times. Even the basic conditions of responsibility to a worker's family, the elementary requirements of rest, leisure, and some semblance of a life outside work, are undermined. And behind all this is a new insecurity of employment. It is because the dockers have decided to stand up against this that their fight evokes solidarity.

But it is here, exactly on these basic and simple issues, that the most ambitious step forward is demanded. Here are

THE NEXT STEPS

questions which face the whole class. They are issues which originate not just in the greed or aggressiveness of this or that employer, nor from the policy of a particular government. They are the inescapable manifestation in everyday life of a structural crisis to which capitalism cannot any longer find compromise solutions. The contradictions of which this crisis consists demand that capital turns inwards, imposing new levels of exploitation, and inevitably resorting to increasingly repressive political means in order to do this. And so the issues now confronting millions of workers mark the beginning (even though they have been building up for some 20 years) of a new way of life and work which capital must impose upon labour.

This must be countered at every stage of the attack through which capital imposes these attacks. And it must be countered by building up a movement which organises the class as a class, that is, not just resisting as the particular group or section which happens to be under attack at any particular time. This means working to build a party of the class.

Because the movement has to develop on these very basic questions, it is clear from the very beginning that the division between the 'industrial' and 'political' wings of the working-class movement has to be consciously overcome. The reason is simple: it is because it is the strength and unity of the working class itself, as a class, that has to be brought to bear to resolve the situation. It is absolutely unacceptable that, in confronting the conditions now being imposed by capital, in reconstructing its class movement in order to do this, the working class should be restricted, politically, to waiting on the electoral and parliamentary decisions of its supposed representatives. The fact is that an essential part of the necessary development of a 'mass communist consciousness' (Marx) without which the achievement of socialism is unthinkable is consciously to oppose and dispense with the whole bureaucratic and parliamentary control hitherto imposed upon it.

On April 27, 1996, the Liverpool dockers held a conference, attended by over 200 people from a wide range of working-class organisations. The following resolution was carried;

THIS Conference recognises that the dispute of the 500 sacked dockers is a struggle which represents the interests of millions of working people nationally and internationally. By defending trade union principles in not crossing a picket line, the Liverpool dockers inspire workers.

The Mersey Docks and Harbour Company are out to smash trade union rights by introducing casualisation, wage cuts, taking away hard-won working rights and conditions. There is an employers' offensive here and internationally.

The dockers' fight is the fight of the working class. Victory for Liverpool dockworkers will be a victory for all workers.

The Merseyside Port Shop Stewards' Committee thanks dockworkers throughout the world who are taking action against shipowners. This world-wide blockade of the port of Liverpool is key to the future victory. It pays thanks to trade unionists throughout Britain who have sustained our struggle — physically, financially and morally — without this our struggle would not have come this far. It recognises the tremendous role of the dockers and their supporters in maintaining the mass pickets from day one of the dispute.

The conference agrees that:

■ The TUC should call a one-day strike — or stay-away from work — in support of the dockers and in opposition to anti-trade-union laws. It should follow the example of the Scottish TUC and establish a hardship fund for the dockers' families.

■ All trades councils be encouraged to pass resolutions along these lines and for support groups to continue with the speaking tours and fund-raising efforts.

■ A national support group structure be set up to assist the dockers and all workers who are in dispute.

■ This network, in conjunction with the Liverpool dockers shop stewards' committee, will decide on national mass pickets and a national demonstration organised in London.

■ Support groups on behalf of the dockers to organise picketing and

leafletting of those firms who continue to ship their goods through Liverpool docks. Support groups to continue action against Drake International and PDP supplying scab labour.
■ Support groups to promote the sales of the pamphlet 'Never Cross a Picket Line', the 'Dockers Charter' and the other items of merchandise.
■ Internationally, a day be established to declare a one-day strike of all longshoremen worldwide in support of the reinstatement of the 500 sacked dockers.

VICTORY TO THE LIVERPOOL DOCKERS!

HERE was a big step forward in the dockers' fight, and potentially for the working class. Much depends on how the resolution is implemented. Because the setting up of such a network can have implications for the whole class movement of the working class, it also demands and makes possible a big step forward in the work for the new party decided on March 16.

The conference held on 16 March to discuss 'The crisis in the labour movement and the need for a new party' resolved to work to broaden the discussion in every region and to organise another conference in October. These are the first necessary steps, to be taken decisively as part of a definite and consciously prepared series of measures over the period leading to the next wave of mass struggles (anticipated in the miners' strike, the anti-poll tax movement, the mobilisations against pit closures, the dockers' and other struggles in 1995-1996) in order that on the basis of that wave a new party will be formed.

Along this road, it is now necessary, at that proposed conference, to found an interim or transitional new political organisation called 'Marxists for a Socialist Party' - or some better name — which expresses that objective. How that new organisation will develop, in relation to the formation soon of a new workers' party based on Marxism, is not a matter of choice. it depends on developments in the economic and political crisis in the coming months, on our study of these and of the experiences of the working-class movement, and on the results of our own work.

To say this is most definitely not to encourage some sort of waiting on events. On the contrary!

Most important of all is a definite and determined orientation, pivoting everything we do on the decided course towards the creation of a revolutionary party. That above all is what the new situation demands.

The necessary general direction is clear, and the main aim we must now resolutely pursue - the founding of a new party - is clear, once we grasp the nature of the new period. The immediate necessary step is to organise this work for the new party, and to found Marxists for a Socialist Party. However, the specific stages through which the class movement of the working class will pass, the way in which this or that issue or struggle will make possible a more significant leap forward or broaden greatly the scope of the movement - these cannot be known in advance. At every point the most serious attention to scientific theoretical study is required, in order to understand the changing situation and the needs of the fight. Marxism is not a fixed doctrine, it is a guide to action. It must be developed, not learned by rote.

In step with the kind of solidarity work outlined above, it is essential to work constantly to bring together all possible resources: technical, literary, journalistic, artistic, scientific and theoretical skills and knowledge, the most advanced communication skills, and so on. All these are vital as we work to increasingly succeed in winning the widest possible support for each and every movement of resistance to the demands of capital - whether it be workers resisting closures, communities resisting cuts in services, protesters against destruction of the countryside, or one of a thousand other movements.

The knowledge and skills of the thousands of highly skilled people such as scientists, technicians, writers, designers, teachers and researchers of all kinds are, in the present system, inevitably subordinated to the requirements of capital.

But in a period of historical crisis such as ours, there are many intellectuals, and there will be more, who find themselves forced to face up to the glaring contradiction between capital's rule and the future of culture, even of humanity itself.

A working-class party does not consist only of workers. It consists of all those who understand that it is the working class which, in emancipating itself, opens the door to the liberation of mankind. It is in the essential work of socialist education, exposing and understanding the destructive workings of capital, arming itself with the necessary strategy to overthrow it, that the working class will find work for the willing hands of all those intellectuals who reject the role assigned to them by capital, and know that they must fight for the socialist future. This work is an absolutely essential element in the work for a new party.

A new and essentially favourable situation has been opened up by the disintegration of Stalinism, the new stage of capitalism's structural crisis, and the definitive end of social-democratic reformism.

The theme of this pamphlet has been that every socialist must be inspired by the opportunity and the responsibility which this change presents to us. In the struggles now unfolding, the class movement of the working class can be reconstructed on new foundations, if only there is conscious work to find ways to open it up to the great new possibilities. For that to happen, the Marxists should understand that, as part of the working class, it is their task also to open up their Marxism to those possibilities.

Appendix I

From Workers Press 20 July 1996

THE BASIC LINES OF OUR WORK

THE WRP congress of the 6-7 July resolved to set up *a new political organisation of all those who are for building a new socialist party of the working class founded on Marxism*. It will be called something like Marxists for a Socialist Party (MSP).

Workers Press is now open for discussion up to and including the November conference to establish the MSP, on the programme, aims and structure of the new organisation.

How we envisage this is that the MSP will be an organisation combining all those who are agreed on the following:

❶ The party the working class needs must be based on *Marxism*.

❷ It will be *internationalist* and international. This means, open to all men and women who agree with its socialist aims and rules, regardless of national origin; and it will aim in all its work at the building of a world party of socialism of which it will be part.

❸ It will be founded on the basic principle that the *emancipation of the working class is the task of the working class itself*. It follows that the *reconstruction* of the working-class movement, so necessary after the definitive failure of Stalinism, of social democracy and Labourism, is the task of the working class itself. The new party is part of that self-reconstruction; not a party 'supplied' to the working class but one built by the working class.

4 It will be a party aiming at the achievement of socialism *not through parliamentary representation* but through the self-organisation and activity of the working class as a class, together with its allies. Parliament is part of the capitalist state, essentially the instrument of control over the working class. For the new party, parliamentary elections and activity are a subordinate part of the class movement of the working class.

5 It will therefore reject the *reactionary division* between the 'industrial' and 'political' arms of the working-class movement. On the contrary, it will aim to bring to bear politically, as a class, the organised, united strength of the working class.

6 It will fight for the end of British rule in *Ireland* and will work with all those who fight for a socialist united Ireland.

7 It will be formed and built not through some amalgamation or 'regroupment' of existing socialist groups, but from all those workers and other socialists who come forward in the struggles of the working class and form its *vanguard*.

8 It will work for the closest relations with, and through its members to influence, all working-class, youth, women's, community and popular organisations and movements. Its members will participate in the struggles and activities of these organisations with the aim of ensuring their growth and *success and their contribution to the building of that unity and consciousness of the class as a whole* which is essential in preparing the decisive struggles for socialism that are ahead.

9 It will therefore at all times work for *united front actions* and movements with the organisations of the working class.

10 It will be a party which *brings together* in a *common strategy and socialist aim* all movements *against capital and its state*.

Building up the forces for the new party

The MSP's members and branches will work to reconstruct and to build up the *solidarity and support networks* from which will come the membership and the organisational framework of this new working-class party. At this point in time, support for the Liverpool dockers' fight is the core of this work.

The MSP will concentrate, in all regions, on *political education and study*, drawing in all those who will take responsibility for the study and development of Marxist theory. (Organising this work will be the responsibility of the research and policy unit decided on by the 'Crisis in the labour movement' conference last March.)

The MSP will direct its work to towards the *organised working class* in the trade unions and also to the organisations of the unemployed, building on the work of the International Trade Union Solidarity Campaign.

The MSP will work to *unite the struggles* of all workers, whatever their national origin, for trade union rights, for wages, working conditions and shorter working hours, and against casualisation and discrimination on any grounds.

BASIC LINES OF OUR WORK

The MSP will work in the closest collaboration with, and seek to unite, all *refugee and liberation movements*, in particular in continuing the international solidarity work of Workers Aid for Bosnia, the fight against the Asylum and Immigration Bills and all immigration controls, against the British government's support of repressive regimes, and against British imperialism's rule in Ireland.

The MSP will carry out *open and intensive propaganda and discussion work* to build for the new socialist party in the course of the coming general election campaign. It will bring into that campaign the struggles of the working class, first and foremost that of the Liverpool dockers, concentrating on the preparation of the working-class movement to deal with the attacks of a 'New Labour' government and its anti-union laws, and on recruiting to the MSP from the Labour Party and the trade unions.

The MSP will set up special working commissions to plan activity directed at organisations and movements of *women and youth*.

The MSP will seek to work with, and to bring into closest relation with the organised working class, *the anti-racist and anti-fascist movements*.

The MSP will support and work shoulder-to-shoulder with all those who come into struggle *to defend communities and the environment* against their exploitation and destruction by capital.

The MSP will work to support and to unite with all those who come into conflict with the capitalist state in defence of the *health* and *education* services and in defence of *democratic rights*.

These are the basic lines along which the WRP is pledged to work for the new organisation, Marxists for a Socialist Party. We put forward these points as a basis for discussion.

A NEW PARTY — WHY? HOW? WHEN

Resolution from 16 March

We republish the main resolution passed at the 'Crisis in the labour movement' conference on 16 March:

This conference resolves that the working class needs a new party for socialism. Now the task is to take the discussion on the programme, organisation and the formation of a new party as widely as possible into the working class.

We affirm that it must be a party *of* the working class, formed out of its struggles, and not a party 'supplied' to the working class.

Conference constitutes a steering committee, open to all present and all who share this common objective.

The next tasks are:

■ To organise in every area a report meeting on this conference.

■ To participate actively in the main struggle of the day, building a network of support committees for the dockers. This network can be the basis of permanent working-class organisation to support such struggles.

The discussion in every area should firstly centre on how to unite the working class on the problems confronting the dockers, and at the centre of this need for unity is the urgent need for a socialist party. Out of the dockers' fight must come the bringing together of the vanguard of the working class in one party.

We must seek every avenue of discussion and united action with members of the Socialist Labour Party and discussion and participation with the Socialist Alliances in various areas.

The steering committee should work to set up a 'Policy Research Unit' to assist in all struggles.

Conference resolves to reconvene in October this year to discuss the next step.

[The Conference has now been booked for Saturday 23 November 1996 at Conway Hall, London.]

Appendix II

Marxism and the working class today
Cliff Slaughter's closing remarks at
WRP Congress 6-7 July 1996

IN working to grasp the nature of capitalism's crisis today and the kind of organisation and consciousness which the working class needs in order to resolve that crisis, we have had to try to re-study and understand the historical contradictions of world capitalism.

Coinciding - of course not at all accidentally - with today's structural crisis of capital is the demise of the Stalinist bureaucracy and of social-democratic reformism, those instruments by which the working class was divided and prevented from achieving its own liberation, that is, its socialist revolution on the world scale.

To grasp today's situation, it is necessary to pose the questions: how did Marx see the future revolutionary victory of the working class? A century and a half later, has his theory been disproved by history? Accordingly, to what extent is Marx's theory the 'guide to action' of the working-class movement? We have tried to show in this booklet what is meant today by the proposition (Marx's) that the only force that can liberate humanity is the working class, which in the process abolishes itself as a class.

Marx wrote in 1845 (in 'The German Ideology'):

> ... a class is called forth which has to bear all the burdens of society without enjoying its advantages, which is ousted from society and forced into the sharpest contradiction to all other classes; a class which forms the majority of all members of society, and from which emanates the

consciousness of the necessity of a fundamental revolution, the communist consciousness, which may, of course, arise among the other classes, through the contemplation of the situation of this class . . .

This communist consciousness - 'of the necessity of a fundamental revolution' - Marx goes on, cannot come into existence on the necessary mass scale except through the revolution itself. That is to say, it is quite mistaken to think that the gaining of communist consciousness on the necessary mass scale can or must be achieved as a prerequisite of the socialist revolution, as some think (such as those who are sceptical today of the possibility of revolutionary politics because of the damage done to working-class consciousness by Stalinism). On the contrary! Marx adds:

Both for the production on a world scale of this communist consciousness, and for the success of the cause itself, the alteration of men on a mass scale is necessary, an alteration which can only take place in a practical movement, a revolution, not only because the ruling class cannot be overthrown in any other way, but also because the class overthrowing it can only in a revolution succeed in ridding itself of all the muck of ages and become fitted to found society anew ('The German Ideology', in Collected Works of Marx and Engels, Vol.5, pp.52-53).

This 'alteration of men on a mass scale' means long and bitter struggles culminating in a successful revolution. Marx obviously could not know, in 1845, how long these struggles would last or what the contradictions in the process would be. It was certainly quite impossible to envisage, in 1845, or at any time in the 19th century, today's world, in which the power of capital, now having established itself in every corner of the globe, threatens not only mass degradation but the very survival of humanity, even of the planet itself, if it is not overthrown by the only antagonist which confronts it as a whole, namely labour, the working class.

Marx wrote about the achievement of the necessary level of 'mass communist consciousness' for a successful revolution through the development of the productive forces made inevitable by capitalism, through the contradictions between these forces and the social relations of capitalism, and the struggles forced on the working class by these contradictions. Through these he was confident that there would grow a worldwide trade unionism ('combination') and the political militancy necessary to confront and defeat capitalism.

We can say now, on the basis of the absolutely necessary analysis of the experiences of the international working-class movement since 1845 and the positing of it against Marx's analysis/prognosis, that the conditions foreseen and prepared for theoretically by Marx and Engels have indeed developed, but through a richly contradictory process which it would be quite foolish to expect them to have foreseen. They saw the future spread of capitalist production and the world market as producing at the same time new millions of wage workers, and they knew that this would mean the organisation of these millions and their growing consciousness of the necessity to fight capitalist exploitation.

In the period since Marx's early writings and his activity in the First International, the working-class movement has certainly become a reality in every country in the world. But there have been differentiations, internal contradictions, divisions and oppositions within that growth. And the superseding or overcoming of these divisions is (and has been for a century now, in different forms) a prerequisite for the growth towards a 'mass communist consciousness' which truly can stand up to and defeat capitalism today.

What this means is that the development of the capitalist system on a world scale up to the present-day 'globalisation', and the development of the struggles, organisation and consciousness of the working-class movement, took very contradictory forms, inevitably; concrete forms which Marx could not know anything about. This is true, even if we take into account, and they are very important, Marx and Engels' severe criticism of the direction of the German workers' movement, and the very insightful letter of Marx to Engels in 1858: 'For us the difficult question is this: the revolution on the Continent is imminent and its character will be at once socialist; will it not be necessarily crushed in this little corner of the world, since on a much larger terrain the development of bourgeois society is still in the ascendant?'

In fact the expansion of capitalism internationally, its establishing of the world market, then the massive export of capital in the imperialist stage and the inter-imperialist rivalries economically, politically and militarily, posed entirely new divisions and problems for the working-class movement.

A massively bigger, international working class came into existence. Millions upon millions of subsistence cultivators and people living in conditions of feudal serfdom or under the heel of 'Asiatic despotisms' were torn from the soil and transformed into landless proletarians and the poorest peasants. And this new, worldwide working class was fragmented, deeply divided, not just separated by geography but by colonial super-exploitation and the buying-off of a stratum of better-off workers and their unions in the main capitalist countries. And this caste, a labour aristocracy, worked and organised in the trade unions and political parties not only against the workers of colonial countries but also against the low-paid, unskilled and unemployed in their 'own' countries. Thus, if there were to develop the global trade unionism and political militancy necessary to get to 'communist mass consciousness' (Marx) it was not going to be a straight-line development but a long battle to overcome their divisions and through this to achieve the necessary integration. A series of long battles against every agency dividing the working class - including its own party and trade union leaders who chose to base themselves on an alliance with their 'own' national ruling class - became absolutely necessary.

The first breakthrough against these reactionary and essentially nationalist divisions came with the Russian Revolution of October 1917, followed immediately by the founding of the Communist (Third) International.

But capitalism was able, after intensive and bitter struggles and repression, to contain this breakthrough, that is, to isolate the Soviet state and eventually to use it (because of the victory of the Stalinist bureaucracy over the Soviet working class, which resulted from its isolation and economic backwardness) as a factor in capitalism's own restabilisation for a whole historical period. While it is correct to see this isolation and economic backwardness of the Soviet Union as the cause of the inability of the workers there to contain and defeat the bureaucracy and to go forward to the construction of socialism, it is absolutely necessary to understand that it was the domination of the workers' movement in the advanced capitalist countries by the social-democratic national reformists (inflicting defeat particularly on the German working class) that made that isolation inevitable.

Once the Stalinist bureaucracy had usurped the political power of the Soviet working class, its counter-revolutionary nature and role was manifested throughout the class struggle from the late 1920s right through to the end of the 1980s. Where national-liberation movements came forward against imperialism, the working class in these movements was subordinated, through Stalinist leadership, to the native capitalists and their parties and armies. The weight of the Soviet state's economic, military and 'security' strength was put behind these bourgeois nationalist leaders, who suppressed any proletarian opposition both before and after independence, in regimes which lived under the 'left' cover of Soviet support and the growth of a so-called 'socialist camp'.

In this way the working class of the colonial and ex-colonial countries (newly named the 'Third World') was further separated from its sisters and brothers in both the advanced capitalist countries and in the Soviet Union, eastern Europe and China. At the same time the Soviet Union was drawn by the bureaucracy into the 'division of the world between the Great Powers' that characterised imperialism. Its control over eastern Europe through bureaucratically deformed states such as the Soviet Union itself, after the 'post-war settlement' with the victorious capitalist powers Britain and the US, in 1945, led not to the advance of socialism, but, on the contrary, to a half-century of separation of the workers of 'the West' and eastern Europe and the USSR, and finally to the restoration of capitalism now in progress.

The international 'federations' of trade unions were instruments of, on the one hand, the Stalinist bureaucracy, and on the other, the CIA.

Considering all these past divisions, all creating conditions in which capitalism could temporarily displace or slow down its historic contradictions, it is now essential to see just how profound are the implications of the collapse of Stalinism, the end of even the semblance of rule through a social reform movement or social democracy, and the completion of imperialism's globalisation and running-out of options.

Out of the century and a half of divisions and differentiations as capitalism expanded on the world arena, the class struggle under capitalism has now arrived at a situation where the coming together of trade unionism internationally with consciousness of the necessity of political struggle by the working class - anticipated by Marx as the process through which arises the necessary 'communist mass consciousness' of socialist revolution - is now insistently posed before the working class. 'Globalisation' creates the maximum interconnections and commonness of problems. It is on this profound basis that we must conclude not just that the situation today is 'complex and contradictory', as some say, but qualitatively new, and favourable (this term is too mild) for the revolutionary reconstitution of the working-class movement.

Furthermore, even the beginnings made in this direction by comrades in our own party and by new forces entering the political struggle point the way forward. It is only necessary to refer to the successful fight for internationalism against all odds in the North-east area of the miners' union, the struggle of comrades in Namibia and in South Africa for independent parties of the Workers International, the enormous effort put into the Workers Aid for Bosnia convoys and the situation now where the reconstruction of the workers' movement in Bosnia has come directly into relation with the fight of the dockers in Britain and the work in Unison, the GMB and other trade unions.

At the centre of this is the successful second international conference of the International Trade Union Solidarity Campaign (ITUSC), whose committee now brings together trade unionists of many nationalities and will become a beacon for the building of class-struggle and internationalist trade unions everywhere.

And so, it becomes possible to understand how the reconstruction of the working-class movement in its basic organisations can be guided only by those who embrace the revolutionary perspective prepared by Marx, at this higher and later level, overcoming the contradictions developed over 150 years. The ITUSC, and the proposal now to work for an intermediate Marxist political organisation towards a new revolutionary party, are the means to implement the founding perspective of the Workers International: the reconstruction of the Fourth International is necessary and possible only in and through the reconstruction of the international working-class movement itself.

Reclaim the Future

We publish below a statement by Reclaim the Streets, whose advance team worked with the Mersey Port Shop Stewards Committee to organise the events on 28-30 September in Liverpool. This was first published in Dockers Charter Anniversary Special, 28 September 1996.

RECLAIM The Future is a convergence of what is mistakenly perceived to be single-issue groups. Anti-road and car protesters, the free party scene, peace groups and workplace struggles are all fighting for the same thing - the removal of a market system which disempowers, destroys the environment, encloses public spaces and removes freedom and responsibility from the individual.

Recognising the need for everyone to have a say in how society is run, we soon come up against those that want to keep decision-making power in the hands of capital. To prevent us from criticising the whole system in its entirety the state uses divide-and-rule tactics. This is why people coming together, unless closely managed by the state, are not allowed - whether it be workers on the picket line or free-partygoers.

As soon as people begin to see the effects of consumer society, whether it be animal, human or ecological exploitation and destruction, they start to fight against these individual manifestations. But everything is interlinked, and a necessary part of the system we are challenging. When we act we must see our struggle in the context of fighting the whole system. The dockers, in particular, have branched out and shown their solidarity with other grassroots movements.

Over the years, while still in work, the dockers have repeatedly refused to handle toxic waste. They have united internationally with other dockworkers who have struck in support and will also be enforcing an international blockade this weekend. We are part of this solidarity with a wide range of groups. We struggle daily against the same source of oppression - the market system. Only as a grassroots movement rejecting reform and compromise, can we realise a free society based on the principles of an ecologically sound society. The state is using its powers to stop this, under the Criminal Justice Act (1994), against striking workers as well as their expected targets in the traveller, squatter and raver communities. Anti-secondary picketing laws were routinely used against protesters at Newbury earlier this year and conspiracy charges have been brought (as yet unsuccessfully) in several cases against alleged organisers of protests and parties.

Meanwhile activists are increasingly suspicious of MI5 involvement in the surveillance of protests and that this role is to be formalised by the threatened Security Services Bill. As politicians gear up to present the electorate with a choice between two virtually indistinguishable political parties, 'Stop the Clampdown - Reclaim the Future' is not merely an expression of mounting disillusion with mainstream politics. It represents a fundamental challenge to the political system.

The groups involved believe that environmental responsibility and quality of life are higher values than the relentless pursuit of profits and economic growth, and personal responsibility and involvement is more important than the politics of the state.